Henry Edward Turner

Greenes of Warwick in colonial history

Read before the Rhode Island historical society, February 27, 1877

Henry Edward Turner

Greenes of Warwick in colonial history
Read before the Rhode Island historical society, February 27, 1877

ISBN/EAN: 9783744717274

Printed in Europe, USA, Canada, Australia, Japan

Cover: Foto ©ninafisch / pixelio.de

More available books at **www.hansebooks.com**

GREENES OF WARWICK

IN COLONIAL HISTORY.

.•.

READ BEFORE THE

RHODE ISLAND HISTORICAL SOCIETY,

FEBRUARY 27, 1877,

BY

HENRY E. TURNER, M. D.

NEWPORT. R. I.:
DAVIS & PITMAN, STEAM PRINTERS.
1877.

GREENES OF WARWICK

IN COLONIAL HISTORY.

READ BEFORE THE

RHODE ISLAND HISTORICAL SOCIETY,

FEBRUARY 27, 1877,

BY

HENRY E. TURNER, M. D.

NEWPORT, R. I.:
DAVIS & PITMAN, STEAM PRINTERS,
1877.

FIRST JOHN GREENE.

FIRST GENERATION.

I propose, Mr. President, with your permission, to present a sketch of the branch of the Greene family, which, as well from its direct descent from the eldest son of John Greene, as from its prominent association with Colonial affairs, and its leading influence in them, may, with propriety, be styled the elder branch, without disparagement to other branches of the same stock, eminently respectable as they were, and frequently active and conspicuous in public affairs. I may say, that the line I speak of were more distinctly and prominently and continuously important in the Colonial and Revolutionary administrations, than any other family can claim to be. And although the transcendent lustre which attaches to the name of Nathaniel Greene, who represents another line of descent from the same source, has, in a measure, cast in the shade those of his kinsmen whose sphere of action was more limited, and whose qualifications were of a very different kind and degree, it may not be a task entirely thankless and fruitless, to pass an hour in discussing the services of his less prominent kinsfolk.

In so doing, I do not propose to set up any claim for them to remarkable brilliancy of genius, or for those marked characteristics which bring a limited number of names into such prominence, in each generation, as to fix the attention of men for all time; nor do I intend to weary you with superlatives and expletives, with the design to magnify their personality by superfluous gilding, but to pass over, in review, such periods of Colonial history as they were intimately associated with and participated in, and in which they were important factors; and to show, (what I verily believe) that during those periods, the democratic principle (I mean thereby, personal liberty and equal rights) was undergoing its crucial tests, and that, in all cases, this race were found, under all risks and at all sacrifices, identified with the party which represented that principle.

I expect to show, instead of the captivating qualities to which I have alluded, the persistent endurance and the persevering determination by which most of the conquests of civilization are attained.

They were distinguished rather by the qualities of the granite, that forms the framework of the everlasting hills, than by those of the plastic material which overlies it, which may be moulded into the most artistic and beautiful forms, and ornamented with the most delicious colors and the most ravishing designs, but whose distinguishing characteristic is fragility; or by those of the glittering products of its seams and interstices.

John Greene, surgeon, was son of Peter of Aukley Hall, Salisbury, Wiltshire, England. He died at Warwick, 1658; his first wife, the mother of his children, died at Conanicut, 1643, having taken refuge there when the Massachusetts troops, under Captain Cooke, made their raid on the defenceless and inoffensive inhabitants of Warwick, or as it was then called Shawomet, and was possibly, and even probably, one of the victims of that monstrous aggression.

His second wife was Alice Daniels, a widow, who was taxed 2s. 6d. for land held in Providence, in 1637. [Col. Rec. 1, 15.]

His third wife, who survived him, was named Philip; an unusual feminine name, probably designed to be Philippa.

He had by his first wife, Joan Tattersall, six children, of whom five survived, one dying in infancy.

First, John, born 1620, baptized August 15, 1620, died November 27, 1708, aged 88 years. Married Ann Almy of William, Portsmouth.

Second, Peter, born 1621, baptized March 10, 1621. Married Mary Gorton of Samuel, Warwick.

Third, James, born 1626, baptized June 21, 1626, died April 27, 1698, aged 71 years. Married, first, Deliverance Potter of Robert, Warwick; second, Elizabeth Anthony of John, Portsmouth.

Fourth, Thomas, born 1628, baptized June 4, 1628, died June 5, 1718, aged 90 years. Married Elizabeth Barton of Rufus, Warwick.

Fifth, Joan, born 1630, baptized October 3, 1630, died young.

Sixth, Mary, born 1633, baptized May 19, 1633. Married James Sweet, and is reputed to be the progenetrix of the well known race of bonesetters.

All these have very numerous descendants, except Peter, who died childless.

According to Savage, John Greene came from Hampton, in the James, April 6, 1635, and arrived at Boston, with wife and five children, June 5, 1635; had been of Salisbury, was at Providence in 1636, went to London in 1644, to negotiate for Narragansett.

According to Drake's researches, John Greene, surgeon, shipped at Hampton, in James of London, April 5, 1635, wife and children not mentioned.

As the name of John Greene does not appear in Massachusetts Colonial Record, in the period intervening between his arrival at Boston and his settlement at Providence, it is to be presumed that he made no settlement in Boston or elsewhere in Massachusetts; we know, however, that he was at one time in Salem, where he probably was associated with Roger Williams; August 1st, 1637, he first appears on Massachusetts Colonial Record in this wise.

2

" Mr. John Greene of New Providence, bound to Quarter Court, first Tuesday of 7th month next, for speaking contemptuously of magistrates, in 100 marks." [Mass. Col. Rec. Vol. 1, p. 200.]

On which the action taken is as follows:

"John Greene of New Providence, fined £20, and forbidden this jurisdiction, on pain of fine and imprisonment, for speaking contemptuously of magistrates, Sept. 19, 1637. [Mass. Col. Rec., Vol. 1, p. 203.]

It appears, from a subsequent record, that John Greene was not as thoroughly impressed with their justice and magnanimity as they thought the circumstances warranted. for March 12, 1638, they have the following entry, viz.:

" Whereas, A letter was sent to this court, subscribed by John Greene, dated from New Providence, and brought by one of that company, wherein the court is charged with usurping the power of Christ over the churches and men's consciences, notwithstanding he had formerly acknowledged his fault, in such speeches, by him before used ; it is now ordered, that the said John Greene shall not come into this jurisdiction, upon pain of imprisonment and further censure ; and because it appears to this court that some others, of the same place, are confident in the same corrupt judgment and practice ; it is ordered that if any others of the same Plantation of Providence shall come within this jurisdiction, they shall be apprehended and brought before some of the magistrates, and if they will not disclaim the said corrupt opinion and censure, they shall be commanded presently to depart out of this jurisdiction, and if such person shall after be found in this jurisdiction, they shall be imprisoned and punished as the court shall see cause." [Mass. Col. Rec., Vol. 1, p. 224.]

There is no record of specific charges against Greene, upon which the action of the Massachusetts court was based, and we are left to inference, as to whether the offence was committed within their bounds, or whether within the limits of Providence, since their conduct on several subsequent occasions proves that the in-

habitants of any part of what constitutes Rhode Island had no
rights which they considered themselves bound to respect; and
the acts of the commissioners of the United Colonies show that
the other colonies which constituted the League endorsed and confirmed their views; and their tenor shows that the spirit which
actuated them had its origin, as much in a purpose to control the
liberal spirit, that inspired the settlers of Rhode Island, Providence
and Warwick, and to prevent their obtaining any recognition, as a
distinct Colony from the government in England, as to provide for
mutual defense against foreign foes and Indian savages.

The circumstance that Greene was bound for trial at a future
term of the Court, proves that he was in custody, and the absence
of evidence that he disputed their power or forfeited his bond,
compels the inference that he submitted; but the vote in the succeeding March shows that they had received a letter from him, in
the interval, of which no record appears, and the tone of which, we
therefore, cannot justly estimate, but we can hardly fail to conclude
that the essential specification, viz.: "Usurping the power of Christ
over the churches and men's consciences," as charged therein, was
thoroughly vindicated by the whole policy of their government,
and especially in their treatment of the settlers in this Colony.

Now, be it observed, that all these things transpired before the
arch heretic, Samuel Gorton's advent to Providence. He, Samuel
Gorton, came to Boston in 1636, was a resident, for a time, at
Plymouth and then was at Rhode Island May 20, 1638 and April
30, 1639. On this occasion then Greene is not to be regarded as
acting under the influence of Gorton, or even in concert with him,
as he did on many occasions afterward; but as indicating that
sturdy English spirit of freedom which burned in the breasts of so
many of our ancestors, and which, like thrice refined metal, came
each time purer from the crucible, and which eventuated in the
grand results in whose fruition we now exult.

However insignificant in the aggregate of historical items this
transaction may appear, it was one of the earliest assertions of en-

tire and absolute freedom of opinion in defiance of either secular
or ecclesiastical authority and one of the scintillations from the
profound, which aided to kindle the flame which is now lighting
the world in its march to universal emancipation, and seems to me
to entitle John Greene to a high place among the apostles of free
thought.

There are no documents extant (that I know), by which we
may judge of his tone of thought, or style of expression, but we
are not to infer (from their close association) that they resembled
those of Samuel Gorton ; he was probably better educated, as also
was Randall Holden.   Gorton boasts, in correspondence with Governor Winthrop, of his inferiority to his adversaries in that respect
(although he is said to have afterwards become an accomplished
scholar), and thanks God therefor ; his style is, certainly, somewhat
obscure in our comprehension, but, I think, most of his contemporaries, in all their polemical disquisitions, might have plumed themselves on their success in illustrating Talleyrand's celebrated maxim,
by using "Language for the concealment of their ideas."

John Greene was a surgeon: of his qualifications and accom-
plishments we have no means of judging ; probably they were respectable, possibly more.   Respectable they must have been, because, at that period, no man was allowed a license to any trade or
calling without legal tests of his acquirements.

I do not intend to go over, in detail, the controversy between
the government of Massachusetts and the settlers of Warwick,
heretofore so ably and exhaustively examined by Judge Staples,
but an account of John Greene would be manifestly incomplete
without some attention to his participation in it.

The settlers at Shawomet or Warwick entertained a view different from their friends at Providence and Rhode Island (and
perhaps, not as consonant with ours at this day): viz.: that no government established by the settlers could have any authority except
through the assent of the home government: and hence, probably,
arose the differences which induced several individuals of Provi-

dence and Rhode Island to unite with Gorton in the settlement of Warwick.

All the acts of the settlers of Rhode Island, until their acceptance of the Parliament's charter, seem to imply that they intended to establish an independent government, on principles democratic and theocratic ; for, in their fundamental act, they make no allusion to Royal or Parliamentary superiority, but commit themselves to the direct guidance of God, and give perpetual grants of land, and pass laws, in the name of the State (not Colony.)

At a General Court holden at Newport, March 16, 1642, it was ordered "That Richard Carder, Randall Holden, Sampson Shotten and Robert Potter, are disfranchised of the privileges and prerogatives belonging to the body of this State, and that their names be cancelled out of the record." Here surely, was an assertion of some of the highest attributes of sovereignty.

At the same session it was ordered, "That if John Weeks, Randall Holden, Richard Carder, Sampson Shotten or Robert Potter, shall come upon the Island armed, they shall be, by the constable (calling him sufficiently aside), disarmed and carried before the magistrate, and there find sureties for their good behaviour; and further be it established, that if that course shall not regulate them or any of them, then a further due and lawful course, by the magistrates, shall be taken, at their session, provided, that this order hinder not the course of law already begun with John Weeks.'

What may have been the offence with which these men were charged we are not informed by the record; it is certain, however, that they were all parties to the deed of Shawomet, from Miantonomi, Jan. 12, 1642. John Greene, Francis Weston, Richard Waterman and John Warner were from Providence, and seem to have been, as he himself expressed it, loving friends of Roger Williams, but they seem to have had differences, not now easily elucidated, which induced them to go beyond Williams' purchase and claim of jurisdiction ; from that time no dispute appears between them and the authorities of Providence and Rhode Island,

3

and in 1649 they became united with them under the charter.
The eleventh grantee of Shawomet was William Woddell, who
was a resident of Portsmouth.

The only records which throw any light on the removal of the
friends of Gorton from Providence to Warwick are, the complaint
of certain residents of Providence to the Massachusetts government, dated Nov. 17, 1641, to which, as Governor Winthrop says,
the reply was, "We had no calling or warrant to interpose in their
contentions, except they did submit themselves to some jurisdiction, either Plymouth's or ours," and some expressions of Roger
Williams, in disparagement of Gorton; but inasmuch as Williams
himself suffered quite as much detraction at the hands of the Massachusetts people, and as the Warwick people contradicted the
imputations upon them in equally strong terms in writing, and also
discountenanced them by their subsequent wise conduct of their
own affairs, and acted harmoniously and successfully with their de-
tractors in Colonial affairs, we may safely conclude, that they were
not more at fault than the others. However that may be, it appears
that they immediately formed the judicious resolution to withdraw
from the neighborhood, and establish an independent community
by themselves; for, whereas, the letter to Massachusetts is dated
Nov. 17, 1641, Miantonomi's deed to them, is dated Jan. 12, 1642,
and there is no evidence afterward of their interfering in the affairs
of their neighbors, or cultivating any differences among themselves,
or of any dissensions other than those incident to all human association; on the contrary, no community on this continent, were
more sedulous in courting the goodwill and confidence of the natives, and none practised more forbearance and endurance under
trials, such as are rarely paralleled. Hardly had they time to provide the rudest shelter for their families and cattle, which the wilderness afforded material for, before the ingenuity of some of their
former neighbors of Providence found means to bring them (in
their helplessness) into conflict with the government of Massachusetts, then the most powerful on the continent, claiming jurisdic-

tion over a vast and comparatively undefined territory, and administered by men who represented the sternest form of Puritanism, and who religiously believed, with a burning sincerity and zeal, that it was their mission to establish the kingdom of God on earth, according to their understanding of it. It is not to be wondered at, that when, in answer to their summons (issued at the instigation of four men of Providence) to the settlers of Shawomet, they received an answer disclaiming their right of interference, expressed in anything but respectful language, and impugning their claims, as representing God's kingdom on earth, they should have been embittered against this little community, groping in darkness, as they regarded it, occupying an insignificant space twenty miles long and four wide on this great continent.

Although the Shawomet settlers refused to subject themselves to Massachusetts on the frivolous pretence of claim set up by them, they very modestly proposed to show their title to such commissioners as Massachusetts might send to them, for that purpose : In answer to which proposition they sent, as commissioners, George Cooke, Edward Johnson and Humphrey Atherton ; and it is worthy of remark, that these same gentlemen were conspicuous as partizans in the future contests, in relation to Indian titles and claims of Connecticut and Massachusetts in King's Province. This is the notification of their appointment :— ᵥ

"To Samuel Gorton, John Wicks, John Warner, John Greene, Randall Holden, Francis Weston, Robert Potter, Richard Waterman, Richard Carder, Sampson Shotten, Nicholas Power, and William Waddle.

"Whereas, upon occasion of divers injuries offered by you to us and the people under our jurisdiction, both English and Indians, we have sent to you to come to our court, and there make answer to the particulars charged upon you, and safe conduct to that end, to which you have returned us no other but contemptuous and disdainful answers, and now, at the last, that if we would send to yourselves, that the course might be examined and heard amongst your own neighbors, we should have justice and satisfaction. We have therefore, that our moderation and justice may appear to all men, agreed to condescend herein to your own desire, and therefor intend shortly to send commissioners into your parts, to lay open the charges against you and to hear your reasons and allegations, and thereupon to receive such satisfaction from you as shall appear, in justice, to be due. We give you also to understand that we shall send a sufficient guard with our commissioners, for their safety against any violence or injury; for seeing you will not trust yourselves with us upon our safe conduct, we have no reason to trust ours with you upon your bare courtesy; but this you may rest assured of, that if you will make good your own offer of doing us right, our people shall return and leave you in peace, otherwise we must right ourselves and our people by force of arms."

Per. Cur.

INCREASE NOWELL, Secretary.

Dated 19th, 7th month, 1643. [Mass. Col. Rec.]

An analysis of this paper will show it to be one of the most grievous travesties of right, justice and law, that ever disfigured the pages of history.

The action of this extraordinary drama commences with the application of four men of Pawtuxet, in the jurisdiction of Providence, and holding land in right of Roger Williams' purchase of Canonicus and Miantonomi, asking to be taken into the jurisdiction of Massachusetts, and submitting themselves thereto, and another from Pumham and Sacononocho, two Indians living at Shawomet and claiming ownership of it, and denying Miantonomi's right to sell it, although Pumham's name is attached to the deed, as a witness. In consequence of these applications the purchasers received a letter requiring them to appear before the Court in Massachusetts to answer the complaint of William Arnold, Benedict Arnold, Robert Cole and William Carpenter.

To which they made answer in a long epistle, dated Nov. 20,

1642, not at all respectful, and abounding in obscure Scriptural allusions, but essentially denying their authority.

"May 10, 1643, Mr. Humphrey Atherton and Mr. Edward Tomlins were appointed by the Massachusetts General Court to go, with Mr. William Arnold, and hold a personal interview with Messrs. Greene, Waterman and the rest."

June 2, 1643, Pumham and Sacononocho, of whom Pumham had signed Miantonomi's deed as witness, submitted themselves to Massachusetts.

How much rum, tobacco and powder, this submission cost, the record does not inform us, we only know, by the record, that these Indians were exempted by special act from the prohibition of the use of powder, which applied to all Indians.

These Indians, who were petty chiefs under Miantonomi, or claimed to be so, claimed the ownership of Shawomet, and a mock trial was had at Boston, no adverse party being present except Miantonomi, the interpreters, as well as the Court, being interested parties ; and as a matter of course, is was determined that the land belonged to Pumham and Sacononocho, and that the Gortonists should be ousted : nor can I find any case before a Massachusetts Court, or the commissioners of the United Colonies, in which Miantonomi or any of his adherents, or the Narragansetts or any of them, were parties, that was not decided adversely to them.

To prove the sincerity of the letter of Sept. 19, 1643, in its assumptions of moderation and justice, I append the proceedings of the Massachusetts General Court, in the period immediately preceding the irruption into Warwick.

[From Mass. Col. Rec., Vol. 2, p. 41.]—"Samu : Gorton and his company had a safe conduct offered them, and were writ unto, about divers injuries offered by them to us (and the people under our jurisdiction, both English and Indians), to come to our Court and there make answer to the particulars, to which they returned no other but contemptuous and disdainful answers, whereupon, three commissioners were resolved to be sent, to require and see

4

satisfaction made, with security, or to bring their persons, with reference to their instructions." Sept. 7, 1643.

[Mass. Col. Rec., Vol. 2, p. 44.]—"It was agreed that we should send three commissioners, with a guard of forty able men to attend them, which have authority and order to bring Samu · Gorton and his company, if they do not give them satisfaction.

\ " The three commissioners are Captain George Cooke, Humphrey Atherton and Edward Johnson; and Captain Cooke to command in chief, and Humphrey Atherton to be his lieutenant of the military force.

" A letter was ordered to be sent to Samu : Gorton and his company, by them which go before, to declare our intent.

" It is ordered that the deputies shall acquaint the elders, to desire, in a special manner, to commend this undertaking to God.

" It is ordered, for the present, that the charge of the soldiers, to go with Captain Cooke, &c., to Providence, should be paid by Mr. Glover and the rest of the committee about the children, and be repaid again when it cometh in.

" It is ordered that Mr. Stoughton and John Johnson, the surveyor, should have warrant to deliver to Captain Cooke, Lieutenant Atherton and Edward Johnson, or any of them, what they desire as needful for themselves or their company." Sept. 7, 1643.

" The Court purposing to adjourn till the eighteenth of the seventh month, and not knowing what may fall out the meanwhile, which may require the authority of this Court, it is therefore ordered, that the magistrates of the Bay, or the greater part of them, and the deputies of Boston, Charlestown, Cambridge, Roxbury, Dorchester, or the greater part of them, shall have power (as a committee), to take order (according to the best discretions) in all the exigents and occasions, which, before the next session of this Court, may fall out, either concerning the expedition now on foot against Sam : Gorton and the rest of that company, or concerning any advice from the commissioners of the United Colonies, about the Narragansett or Mohegan sachems and their people, so as, they are not to enter upon any war with the Indians (other than defensive), before this Court be again assembled." Sept. 7, 1643.

[Mass. Col. Rec., Vol. 2, p. 47.]—"It was ordered that Mr. Stoughton pay £20 to the soldiers, of the stock in his hand." Oct. 17, 1643.

"It is ordered that Pumham and Sacononocho should have, each of them, lent them, a fowling piece, and Benedict Arnold hath liberty to supply them powder and shot as he seeth occasion." Oct. 17, 1643.

"It is ordered, Lucy Pease, wife of ——— Pease, appearing and professing that she doth abhor and renounce Gorton's opinions, and confessing her fault in blotting out some things in the book which she bought, and showing the same before she had delivered it, and professing she was sorry for it, she was dismissed for the present, to appear when she shall be called for." Oct. 17, 1643.

"The charge of the prisoners, Samu: Gorton and his company.

"Upon much examination and serious consideration of your writings, with your answers about them, we do charge you to be a blasphemous enemy of the true religion of our Lord Jesus Christ and His holy ordinances, and also, of all civil authority among the people of God, and particularly in this jurisdiction." Oct. 17, 1643.

What shall we say of the moderation and justice which they wish "to appear to all men," and which induces them "to condescend" to send commissioners to hear the cause (already prejudged), and to receive such satisfaction as shall appear, in justice, to be due; when, previously to inditing the letter in which those expressions appear, they had passed a vote, directing their commissioners, "To bring Samuel Gorton and company to Boston, if they do not give satisfaction;" which duty they performed, without the least pretence of investigation, by the aid of forty soldiers (a greater number, probably, than composed the whole settlement), which they were directed to take with them for that purpose?

The commission of these men does not appear (or whether

they were more explicit than the vote, and directed the victims to be brought, dead or alive), but we are warranted in supposing that all their acts were justified by it; especially as there was no censure of them, and as the acts of the Court afterward exceeded theirs in enormity. They, probably anticipating the policy of the great Napoleon, ordered their troops to subsist upon the enemy, not knowing, however, that their illustrious example, in dealing with their fellow exiles from England, and afterwards with the poor Indians, would receive the seal of the German empire, in their settlement with the French, in the nineteenth century. Subsequent acts of the General Court direct, that their cattle shall be seized and sent to Boston to be sold, for the payment of the expenses of the campaign, and of their trial and imprisonment. [See Mass. Col. Rec., Vol. 2, p. 53.]

Having marched through Providence, regardless (as far as appears) of the right of neutrality, they appeared in Warwick, Sept. 28, .1643, and besieged the men remaining, in a house in which they had taken refuge, and where they, passively, defended themselves, that is (as Samuel Gorton says), without firing a shot, and where they finally capitulated, on condition of going to Boston as friends and neighbors, that is, on parole. In violation of this agreement, they marched them to Boston in chains; and all their treatment afterward was such as is accorded by civilized nations, not to prisoners of war, but to convicted felons: and it was only by two votes (as Samuel Gorton says), that they escaped the penalty of death.

What was their condition of mind, we may judge, when we reflect that their families were scattered about the country, in a rigorous New England Winter, without any provision, their stock driven off by their persecutors or stolen by unfriendly Indians, and their farmsteads ransacked and laid waste by Indians, as well as by their no less unfriendly neighbors of their own race. Only the kindness of their friends at Providence and Rhode Island saved their wives and children from utter extermination; they owed nothing to the tender mercy of their persecutors.

[For Samuel Gorton's account of these transactions, see Staples' Simplicity's Defence, p. 102 et seq.]

It is worthy of notice that Edward Johnson, one of these (so styled) commissioners, as the Gortonists very properly denominated them, was the author of that remarkable tract entitled, "The Wonder Working Providence of Zion's Saviour in New Eng'and " (in which this affair may be studied, from their point of view) ; a work which breathes nothing but glorification of the hierarchical government of Massachusetts, couched in terms almost amounting to blasphemy and fierce denunciations, not only of those who resist, but of all who presume to disapprove any of their arbitrary and tyrannical acts   An extract from it, giving an account of this very transaction, is a pretty good commentary on the judicial fairness to be looked for from that board.

[Johnson's narrative.]—" For not long before, those persons that we spoke of, who encouraged Miantonomi to this war, and with the help of him, enforced Pumham and Sacononocho to set their hands to a writing, which these Gortonists had framed, to take their lands from them ; but the poor sachems, when they saw they were thus gulled of their land, would take no pay for it, but complained to the Massachusetts government, to whom they had subjected themselves and their lands : as also at this time, certain English inhabiting those parts, with the Indians' good leave and liking, desired to have the benefit of the Massachusetts government, as Dover formerly had done, to whom this government condescended, in hope they might increase to such a competent number of godly Christians, as there might be a church of Christ planted ; the place being capable to entertain them in a comfortable measure for outward accommodations; but hitherto it hath been hindered by these Gortonists and one of Plymouth, who forbade our people to plant there. These persons, thus submitting, came at this time also to complain of certain wrongs done them by these Gortonists, who had thus encroached and began to build on the Indians' land. Upon these complaints, the governor and the hon-

5

ored Mr. Dudley issue forth their warrant to summon them to appear, they being then about five or six persons, without any means of instructing them in the ways of God, and without any civil government to keep them in civility or humanity, which made them to cast off, most proudly and disdainfully, any giving account to man of their actions, no not to the chiefest in authority, but returned back most insolent, scornful, scurrilous speeches. After this, the government of the Massachusetts' sent two messengers on purpose to persuade them to come and have their cause heard, assuring them like justice, in their cause, with any other. But Samuel Gorton, being the ringleader of the rout, was so full gorged with dreadful and damnable errors, the which he had newly ensnared these poor souls with, that soon after the departure of the messenger he lays aside all civil justice, and instead of returning answer to the matter in hand he vomits up a whole paper of beastly stuff, one while, scoffing and deriding the ignorance of all, beside himself, that thinks Abraham, Isaac, etc., could be saved by Jesus Christ, who was after born of the Virgin Mary, another while, mocking at the Sacraments of Baptism and the Lord's Supper, in an opprobrious manner deriding at the elements Christ was pleased to institute them in, and calling them necromancers that administer them at all; and in a word, all the ordinances of the Gospel, abominable idolatry he called and likened them to Moloch and the star of the idol Remphan; his paper was thrust full of such filthiness that no Christian ear could hear them without indignation against them, and all was done by him in a very scornful and deriding manner, upbraiding all that use them: in the meantime magnifying his own glorious light, that could see himself to be personally Christ, God-man, and so all others that would believe as he did. This paper he got to be subscribed with about twelve or thirteen hands, his number of disciples being increased, for assuredly the man had a very glossing tongue, but yet, very deceitful; for when he had but a few with him, then he cried out against all such as would rule over their own species, affirming that the

Scriptures term such to be gods of the world, or devils; but after his return from England, having received some encouragement from such as could not look into the depth of his deceit, being done at so large a distance, he getting into favor again with those who had formerly whipped him out of their company, turns devil himself. The godly Governors of the Massachusetts, seeing this blasphemous bull of his, resolved to send forty persons, well appointed with weapons of war, for apprehending of him; who, accordingly, with some waiting, did apprehend him with the rest of his company, except two or three which ran away, without any hurt to any person, although he gave out very big words, threatening them with blood and death so soon as they set foot on the ground; and yet this brazen faced deceiver published in print the great fear their women were put unto by the soldiers; whereas, they came among them day by day, and had it not been that they intended peaceably to take them, they would never have waited so long upon their worships as they did, but being apprehended, and standing to that they had written, yet would they willingly have covered it with some shifts, if they could. The greatest punishment they had was to be confined to certain towns for a few months, and afterwards, banished; but, to be sure, there be they in New England that have Christ Jesus and his blessed ordinances in such esteem, that, the Lord assisting, they had rather lose their lives than suffer them to be thus blasphemed, if they can help it. And whereas some have favored them, and endeavored to bring under blame such as have been zealous against their abominable doctrines, the good God be favorable to them, and prevent them from coming under the like blame with Ahab; and yet they remain in their old way, and there is somewhat to be considered in it, to be sure, that, in these days, when all look for the fall of Antichrist, such detestable doctrines should be upheld, and persons suffered, that exceed the Beast himself in blasphemy; and this to be done by those that would be counted reformers, and such as seek the utter subversion of Antichrist."

Judge Staples comments on this, as follows :—

"Can one be surprised, that the Gortonists refused to have the complaints against them tried by Massachusetts, when the author of the foregoing chapter, was selected by that government, as a commissioner to examine into them? If he was chosen, as a proper person to commend 'the moderation and justice of Massachusetts,' were they not justified in refusing it?"

Previous to the commencement of the leaguer, Gorton and his friends offered to submit the dispute to the King's government *see errata →* commissioners to say, that they suspended operations until a messenger could go to and return from Boston for directions, who returned with an unfavorable answer. This we have, on the statement of Gorton, and, so far as I know, his representations of facts have never been impeached, and had they been, it is amply confirmed by a letter from four men of Providence addressed to Governor Winthrop, dated Oct. 2, 1643, and signed,

CHAD BROWN.

THOMAS OLNEY.

WILLIAM FIELD.

WILLIAM WICKENDON.

Of these, Field and Wickendon had signed the letter to Massachusetts complaining of Gorton, etc., Nov. 17, 1641.

[For this letter, see Staples' Simp. Def., p. 105, et seq.]

This letter is couched in perfectly respectful language, and does great credit to the hearts and intelligence of its senders ; to this, they received a characteristically arrogant reply, the most noticeable clause in which I quote :—

" To yourselves, whom we know not, but have just cause to fear, in respect of your vicinity unto them, and your now mediation for them, and to those of Rhode Island, divers of whom we know too well to refer any matters unto." Signed,

JO. WINTHROP.

[See Staples' Simp. Def., p. 109, et seq.]

This hit at Rhode Island seems to have been an entirely gratuitous ebullition of spleen, but it is of great value, as being one of those faint rays which aid in elucidating the feeling of Massachusetts, and the springs of her action in dealing with our fathers.

I wish to call your attention, for a moment, to an expression of the Massachusetts Court in the vote on the enlargement of the prisoners, March 7, 1644. They are to be enlarged, "Provided, that if they, or any of them, shall, after fourteen days after such enlargement, come within any part of our jurisdiction, either in the Massachusetts, or in or near Providence or any of the lands of Pumham or Sacononocho, or elsewhere in our jurisdiction."

Observe the cunning of this, as well as its arrogance. Although they had marched their army through Providence, going and returning, with baggage and plunder, and sent their officials, and taken the cattle through also, of which they had robbed the poor settlers of Shawomet, this, so far as I am informed, is the first intimation of their having any pretence of claim to Providence. Their claim to jurisdiction in Warwick was founded on a vote of the Commissioners of the United Colonies, which recognized the title to be in Plymouth, and authorized Massachusetts to accept the guardianship of it in case Plymouth refused it, which she did; she considered her title problematical, but was willing, as it then appeared (although she afterwards withdrew from that position), to allow Massachusetts "to pull the chestnuts out of the fire." This question, if time and space allow, I propose to examine more at large hereafter.

It may seem that, John Greene's name not appearing among the captives of Captain Cooke's bow and spear, I had dwelt unnecessarily on this subject; but I regard the three men who escaped capture as equally sufferers with the others, inasmuch as they were put under the ban of outlawry by name, and their property sequestered in the same terms.

Greene, probably, was at Conanicut or Newport ministering to his wife, who died at this time: if she was at Conanicut, as tradition has it, she must have been indebted to the hospitality of the

6

Indians, since Conanicut was sold to William Coddington, Benedict Arnold et al. in 1656, thirteen years later, by Caganaquant.
In all the transactions in Warwick he was a prominent figure, enjoying, fully, the confidence of his fellow citizens, and suffering, in common with them, from the machinations of their enemies in Massachusetts.

It is a singular coincidence, that the withdrawal of the Pawtuxet people from their feigned subjection to Massachusetts, and their release from it, and the death of John Greene, occurred in the same year, 1658.

In the interval between 1643 and 1658 the inhabitants of Warwick enjoyed no repose from the depredations of Pumham and his satellites on the one hand, and the white malcontents on the other, both encouraged by Massachusetts, and justified by her in every sort of irregularity ; it is unnecessary for me to weary you with all the evidence of this, but the letter from Providence Plantations to Massachusetts, of date May 12, 1658, signed Roger Williams, President, which is corroborative of the representations of the Warwick people, asking redress, presents a vivid picture of their sufferings and struggles. [See R. I. Col. Rec., vol. 1, p. 341; also vol. 1, p. 322.]

On the seventh of September, 1643, the Massachusetts General Court voted as follows (after making preparations for the inroad upon the Shawomet settlement), viz.:—

"It is ordered, that the deputies shall acquaint the elders to desire, in a special manner, to commend this undertaking to God."

It is almost impossible to believe (looking from any point within our compass), that these men were sincere in thus asking the blessing of the Most High on an enterprise conceived in sin, and to be prosecuted by carrying the sword and torch into the midst of a poor, feeble and helpless settlement, composed of refugees for conscience sake like themselves, which had only had an existence of little more than a year, which already had all the evils of wild lands and savage neighbors and distant sources of supply to encounter, and whose recent escape from the persecutions of the Mother land, in common with themselves, would seem to have insured their sympathy and aid. Their real motives, in this most unrighteous enterprise, can be attributed to no higher impulses than ambition and greed, and to secure control of those dangerous people who propagated the heretical and damnable doctrine of independent belief and thought.

It was in this year, 1643, that the colonies of Massachusetts, Plymouth, New Haven and Connecticut, established the congress called the Commissioners of the United Colonies, and to which parties from Rhode Island repeatedly asked admission for her and were, as often, repulsed. Ostensibly the object of this association was the common defence. Why then were the inhabitants of Rhode Island denied its advantages? Manifestly, because they regarded Rhode Island as their common enemy; she had obtained recognition from, and owed allegiance to, the same government of Great Britain, and could rightly have no enemies and no allies but such as were equally theirs. They may also have had some doubt whether their aggressive Indian policy would meet with cordial support from the settlers of Rhode Island.

The history of the United Colonies is a history of perpetual efforts, on the part of that organization, to retard and discourage, and if possible to suppress, the Narragansett Plantations.

The first session of this body was in May, 1643, at which Plymouth was not represented; in October of the same year Plymouth was present. Was it necessary to whip Plymouth in? Plymouth was always milder, in her Puritanism, than Massachusetts; she hung no Quakers, she whipped no Baptists, she strangled no witches. Connecticut was the nursling of Massachusetts, was settled by her capital, and her government was conducted, chiefly, by men drawn from her leading families and rejoicing in identical surnames. Was it not a promising scheme, to plant their feet on each side of Narragansett Bay, to strike across its centre, dividing those hotbeds of pestilent heretics Rhode Island and Providence, and then eventually absorb them ? as they must have done, crushed as between the upper and nether millstone ; but the Lord, whom they had profanely invoked, had ordained otherwise.

I have dwelt on the affairs of Shawomet, more perhaps, than it may appear I ought, because I believe this episode in our history does not receive the consideration its importance warrants. To you, students of history, I have presented no facts not already familiar, but to the mass of readers, if they have read them at all, they present nothing but a scrap of local history, of interest, chiefly, as others, to the denizens of such locality. To me it presents a deeper and a wider and a loftier appeal ; an appeal to my pride as a citizen of Rhode Island, and to my gratitude and admiration as a friend of my kind. I regard it also as a key to the whole policy of the other colonies toward Rhode Island. If, as we fondly flatter ourselves, the settlers of Rhode Island were the pioneers in the pathway to freedom of the soul, if they founded the first commonwealth which recognized that great principle, as they undoubtedly did, and if the establishment of that principle, as the fundamental basis of every enlightened government, may, in any measure, be due to our success : then, I say, that we cannot too warmly cherish the memory of those men who resisted the aggressions of Massachusetts ; we cannot too highly appreciate the sturdy will (dogged, if you please), of Samuel Gorton and his associates, who, with chains about their limbs, with the rope imminent about their necks, with desolated firesides, with plundered garners, with households wandering, defenceless, possibly starving, and absolutely dependent on the charity of a needy community, in fine, with the iron penetrating their souls at every point, refused to abjure their manhood.

In pursuance of their hostility to the Narragansett Plantations the authorities of Massachusetts prosecuted, either directly or through their Indian allies, a constant system of spoliation of the Narragansett tribe, whose grand old Sachem Canonicus, and the noble young Miantonomi, were the firm and fast friends of the

Narragansett Bay settlers, to whom they had sold their lands, which were honestly paid for.

Having dissolved the supremacy of the Narragansetts over the Wampanoags, who were their subjects, they made war on them in 1643, in alliance with the Mohegans on various frivolous pretences ; they received Miantonomi (who had been taken by the Mohegans), as prisoner, and condemned him to death ; but, with a sense of shame, for which they are entitled to some credit, they transferred him to Uncas for execution.

The pretexts upon which they found Miantonomi worthy of death were puerile in the extreme, his real crime was his friendship for the settlers of Rhode Island. This subject is admirably disposed of in Staples' Annals of Providence.

Notwithstanding the evident designs of Massachusetts and the circumstances of their own banishment from it, there were not wanting those in Rhode Island who sympathised with Massachusetts in the persecution of their afflicted fellow citizens, and it is a severe stigma on the name of Governor Coddington that he should have come down to us as their mouthpiece in a letter to Governor Winthrop, dated May 25, 1648, as follows :—

" Sir, this bearer Mr. Ballston, and others of this Island, are in disgrace with the people of Providence, Warwick, and Gorton's adherents on the Island, for that we will not interpose or meddle at all in their quarrels with the Massachusetts and the rest of the colonies ; and do much fear that Gorton will be a thorn in their and our sides, if the Lord prevent it not : but I hope, shortly, to see you and to speak with you, and therefore shall, for the present, cease from writing, but not from remaining

Yours ever,

WM. CODDINGTON."

Extract from letter of R. Williams to John Winthrop, jun. (1648 probably), from Cawcumsqussick :—

" Our poor country is in civil dissension, their last meeting (at which I have not been) have fallen into factions, Mr. Codding-

7

ton and Capt. Partridge, &c., the heads of one, and Capt. Clarke (Jeremiah), Mr. Easton, &c., the heads of the other faction; I receive letters from both, inviting me, &c., but I resolve (if the Lord please) not to engage unless with great hopes of peacemaking : the peacemakers are the sons of God." [Winthrop papers, Mass. Hist. Col., vol. 9, p. 278.]   Signed,

R. WILLIAMS.

At the first election, under the Providence charter, 1647, Mr. John Coggeshall was chosen President, at the next, May 1648, Mr. Coddington was elected; nine days after, the letter to Governor Winthrop was written. At the same session, May 16, 1648, Mr. Coddington was suspended for charges, and Mr. Jeremy Clarke elected to serve until the President should be cleared or another elected. Mr. Coddington left for England in January 1649, and before Nov. 1651, had returned with a commission constituting him Governor for life over the Island, probably with the understanding that the reversion of the office should be in his family.

What the charges against Coddington were we do not know, as the records give us nothing more, but he was not reinstated in his office, and his future record shows that he never recovered the confidence of his fellow citizens in the degree he had formerly enjoyed it. In May 1656, he was elected Commissioner from Newport, and it appears from the action of the Assembly at that time. that objections were made to him on account of differences still pending, in England ; and the Assembly sent a letter to Mr. John Clarke (then in England), showing that Mr. Coddington had made his peace with them. At the same session they refuse to return to him a fine " about the record," and, Resolved " to cut out of the Record Book certain transactions which were in the time of Mr. Coddington, his government, and stood in our Book of Record, which might seem prejudicial to himself or others, it being much considered, in the case, this Court not thinking it fit to meddle with it, ordered, that it should be cut out from our Book (which was done), and then delivered to Mr. Coddington.

All which was a great mistake, on the part not only of the Assembly but of Mr. Coddington, inasmuch as we can draw no inference but one unfavorable to him. In all cases the destruction of a record, is a crime, in this case (to use a hackneyed expression) " Twas worse than a crime, 'twas a blunder."

Coddington was Assistant in 1666, and Governor in 1674 and '75, and was elected Governor to complete the term of Benedict Arnold, who died Aug. 28, 1678 ; Coddington died Nov. 1, 1678.

It is impossible to avoid the conclusion, that Coddington procured his commission without authority from his fellow citizens and contrary to their wishes, either to gratify his own ambition or from undue influence on the part of their arch enemy Massachusetts, whose interest was plainly subserved by any dissensions in Rhode Island ; and although, at a less trying period, they magnanimously forgave him, the experiment was fatal to his prestige.

In all the acts of and relating to Warwick, during his life, the name of John Greene rarely fails to occur, and generally second to Gorton's, who was, undoubtedly, the master spirit, Greene and Holden being, perhaps equally, his chosen confidantes ; of the two latter Greene was much the elder.

From the Colonial Record, it appears that he was Commissioner (equivalent to Representative), from 1652 to 1658, when he died ; also in 1651 in the Assembly of Providence and Warwick. From 1651 to 1653 either he or his son acted as General Recorder and Clerk, probably the son, as the signature is sometimes John Greene and sometimes John Greene, jun.

SECOND JOHN GREENE.

John Greene, junior, more familiarly known as Deputy Governor John Greene, died Nov. 27, 1708, aged 88 years. He was born, 1620. His wife was Anne, daughter of William Almy of Portsmouth; she died, May 17, 1709, aged 88 years. Their children were:—

First, Deborah; born August 10, 1649, married William Torrey.

Second, John; born June 6, 1651, no issue.

Third, William; born December 6, 1652, married Mary Sayles, of John.

Fourth, Peter; born February 7, 1654-5, married Elizabeth Arnold, of Stephen.

Fifth, Job; born August 27, 1656, married Phebe Sayles, of John.

Sixth, Philip; born October 7, 1658, married 1st, Dickerson, 2d, Caleb Carr, Jamestown.

Seventh, Richard; born February 8, 1660, married Ellen Sayles.

Eighth, Anne; born March 19, 1662-3, married Thomas Greene, son of Thomas.

Ninth, Catharine; born August 15, 1665, married Charles
Holden.

Tenth, Audrey; born December 26, 1667, married Dr. John
Spencer.

Eleventh, Samuel; born January 30, 1669-70, married Mary
Gorton, of Benjamin, was father of first Governor
William Greene.

He had arrived, then, at man's estate, when the purchase of
Shawomet was made in 1642. His name does not appear in the
deed, except as witness, but it does in some of the acts of Massachusetts General Court, associated with his father's, and also in
division of lands in Providence in 1638, although, at that time, he
must have been a little short of his majority.

In 1651 he was elected Commissioner from Warwick, and was
annually reelected, or rather semi-annually, as was then the practice, until 1659, when he was elected Assistant, and continued so
to be every year, with two exceptions, until 1686, when the charter
was suspended by King James II. He was again elected Assistant in 1689, and in 1690 as Deputy Governor, which office he held
until 1700, a period of 10 years, a longer time than any other person occupied that position in the colonial government continuously and longer than any man was Governor, except Samuel Cranston, who was Governor 30 years, from 1698 to 1727 inclusive. The
lapses in his service as Assistant, probably, were in those years
when he was absent in England on business of the colony; in
1651-2, he was Recorder, and in 1657-8-9 and 61, he was Attorney
General.

In 1654 he was associated with Ezekiel Holliman as a committee to revise the laws, and in Oct. 1664, he was again on a commission for the same purpose with John Clarke, Roger Williams,
John Sanford and Joseph Torrey.

At the session of the Assembly, June 29, 1670, he was appointed "(in case the Governor Benedict Arnold decline the service,)
with John Clarke, physician, to go to England, to vindicate the

8

charter, before the King." Neither Governor Arnold or John
Greene appear to have accepted this service.

A letter appears, dated Feb. 3, 1678-9, in R I. Col. Řec., vol.
3, p. 37, addressed to the Lords of Trade and Plantations, in relation to Mount Hope, signed, Randall Holden and John Greene,
from which it appears they were in London at that time on colonial business, and were consulted on that business as one familiar to
them ; I shall hereafter refer to an important result of the commission then entrusted to them. In July of the same year a rate was
assessed to raise £60 for their expenses to and in England, and in
October 1705 an amount of £30 is allowed to Major John Greene,
for a debt due from the colony for services done in England ; as
this is twenty-five years later, no doubt he had been in England
subsequently.

From 1683 to the time of Andros he was Major of the Main,
equivalent to our Major General.

In October 1664 he was joined in a commission with John
Clarke and Joseph Torrey, to meet commissioners from Connecticut, to settle the boundary, for which he was allowed, March 30,
1671, £10. He was also on a commission to the same purpose in
1670, a mass of records relating to which may be found in R. I.
Col. Rec., vol. 2, p. 309 to 328. In this his associates were Joseph
Torrey and Richard Bailey.

March 13, 1676, he is invited, with sixteen other prominent
citizens, to attend the session of the Assembly, " to advise in these
troublesome times and straites."

June 7, 1671, he was again commissioned, with Deputy Governor Benedict Arnold, John Clarke, John Cranston and Joseph
Torrey, to settle differences with Connecticut.

" March 1, 1664, ordered, that the Governor (B. Arnold), Mr.
Greene, Mr. Card and Mr. Sanford be desired to draw up their
thoughts concerning a Preface or Prologue to the proceedings of
the present Court " (the first held under the charter).

His name is also mentioned in the charter, as one of those "principal persons" applying for it.

September 4, 1666, the Governor (William Brenton), William Baulston, William Harris, Captain John Greene and Mr. John Clarke, are appointed to draw up an address to His Majesty and letters to the Lord Chancellor and Colonel Cartwright.

June 7, 1671, he was on a committee to draw up an answer to the government of Plymouth.

In May 1664, John Greene and Joseph Torrey were appointed commissioners, "to make a treaty with Massachusetts, according to their proposals." Their commission may be seen, R. I. Col. Rec., vol. 2, p. 50.

But I need not cite more evidences of the esteem in which John Greene was held by his associates and the public. The records during his public service of fifty years teem with them, and are very strong presumptive evidence that the severe animadversions of Lord Bellamont and Governor Cranfield are expressions rather of partizan feeling than of judicial conviction.

In pursuance of their usual grasping policy, the Commissioners of the United Colonies laid claim to every part of the territory that now constitutes Rhode Island.

Notwithstanding that, Governor Winslow of Plymouth had advised Mr. Williams, at the time he had taken refuge at Seekonk, to remove across the river, lest, Seekonk being in their jurisdiction, their friends in Massachusetts might take offence; and notwithstanding that, as Mr. Williams says in his letter to the Massachusetts General Court, October 5, 1654, "he had begun that Plantation, by advice of Mr. Winthrop;" Massachusetts repeatedly, and also the Commissioners of the United Colonies asserted their claim to jurisdiction over it, and Massachusetts exercised those rights which she claimed, at least in the terms of banishment of Gorton and his friends. Plymouth also frequently asserted that Rhode Island was within the limits of her patent.

A few words now in relation to the logic of Massachusetts'

claim to Warwick. Although there are occasional intimations of a
direct claim, on the part of Massachusetts, which are conclusively
contradicted by her bounds as described in her patent, her plea, at
all times, was the assent of Plymouth, which assent the Commissioners for Plymouth repudiated and denied, on the part of any
persons having authority from that colony, September 16, 1651 ;
and also the authority of the Commissioners of the United Colonies.

The direct claim of Massachusetts is too flimsy to deserve dis-
cussion : her patent gives her three miles south of Charles river,
or the southernmost point of it, and westward indefinitely on that
line, which is the present north line of Connecticut and Rhode
Island, and by no possible construction could it be tortured to
mean anything south of it.

The grant to Plymouth again, as they very well knew, could
in no way be forced so as to give them any rights of territory any-
where west of the east shore of Narragansett Bay, nor did they
ever attempt to enforce any such claim.

· But suppose that Plymouth had grounds for such a claim,
by what rule of law could she divest herself of any territory per-
taining to her patent, excepting by the surrender of it to the
sovereign authority from which she derived it?

Again, supposing she had that power, how could Massachusetts, whose existence depended on her patent, which explicitly de-
fined her limits and gave no power to extend them, pretend as in
the case of Warwick, on the plea of voluntary subjection and release by Plymouth, and afterward, as in Narragansett, on the plea
of conquest, to exercise sovereign power outside the limits of her
patent ?

Again, how could the Commissioners of the United Colonies,
who had no existence recognized by the parent government, and
no status except what was voluntarily accorded them by the colonies, who had, in point of fact, no legal existence at all, presume
to exercise any authority whatever in this matter ?

The hiatus in the records of Rhode Island, from 1650 to 1653, makes it more difficult than usual to elucidate the divisions which it is evident existed in Newport and Portsmouth, and probably in the other Narragansett settlements in a minor degree. We have seen that some of the settlers of Providence submitted themselves to Massachusetts in 1643, and were never divested of a nominal allegiance to her until 1658. We can easily imagine that they were not, during that interval, in full sympathy with those who desired the independence of Rhode Island; they were, probably, a thorn in the side of the other party, as Governor Coddington hints in his letter to Governor Winthrop, that the friends of Gorton will be in that of his party, which prediction was justified, when three years later, after seven or eight months trial of his government, the people of the Island revolted, and Coddington had to flee for safety. [See Francis Brinley's chronological account, Mass. Hist. Col., 1st Ser., vol. 5, p. —.]

At the meeting of the Commissioners of the United Colonies, September 1648, a petition was received from William Coddington and Captain Partridge, claiming to represent the major part of the inhabitants of Rhode Island, and requesting that the Island might be received into a league of friendship and amity, &c., with all the other colonies, ignoring, as you observe, Providence and Warwick, with which they had united the previous year under the charter of 1643.

The answer to this application was, that their desire might be gratified, by their submitting themselves to Massachusetts or Plymouth, which was exactly what they intended and desired, and only the opposition of the popular party prevented, and was what the whole policy of the United Colonies had contemplated. Observe, that this occurred four months after the suspension of Coddington, and is, without doubt, the key to the popular dissatisfaction. [See Acts Commiss. Uni. Col., vol. 1, p. 210.]

Mr. Coddington, as you recollect, was suspended from his functions as President in May 1648, and never resumed them, the

9

records, as you remember, were afterward expurgated, and we have only collateral evidence for about four years.

About this time Mr. Williams in his letter to John Winthrop, junior, says, "Our poor colony is in civil dissension, their last meetings have fallen into factions, Mr. Coddington, Captain Partridge, &c., the heads of one, Captain Clarke and Mr. Easton, &c., the heads of the other faction."

It is evident from this that there were severe squabbles, and from the short period of Governor Coddington's supremacy under his perpetual commission, and their again uniting with Providence and Warwick, in 1653, that the major part of the inhabitants of the Island, were not his partizans, that on the other hand, the party or faction represented (as Williams indicates) by Captain Clarke and Mr. Easton were the numerically stronger, and after events show that it was this party which sustained popular rights at all times, that they struggled throughout that century against the encroachments of prerogative, as well as against the machinations of the surrounding colonies, and that they finally and triumphantly accomplished the liberation of Rhode Island, and through infinite discouragements, preserved her territorial limits. To this party the Greenes and Holdens of Warwick were as a stay of steel.

The bone of contention, which most occupied the attention of that generation was the jurisdiction and ownership of King's Province or Narragansett Country, now Washington county ; which was claimed by Massachusetts, Connecticut and Rhode Island. In the contentions in relation to it John Greene is always a prominent figure, but in looking into this subject great care is necessary, to avoid confusing his name with that of another John Greene, who was a resident of Narragansett and a partizan of Connecticut, and therefore was in diametrical opposition to him.

The Pequots, by an alliance with the Narragansetts and Mohegans, having been conquered and their tribal power extinguished, their lands, lying chiefly in the valley of the Thames, after a long dispute between Massachusetts and Connecticut, were finally as-

signed to Connecticut as conquered territory, and the remnant of
the tribe were distributed as slaves, the larger part to the Mohegans, the smaller number to the Narragansetts and their tributa-
ries, they paying to the English United Colonies a fixed sum in
wampum, as a tribute for each Pequot, in other words, hire for
services.

The next step necessary was to find or create a pretext for the
like treatment of the other tribes ; and the Narragansetts having
committed the indiscretion (to use a mild phrase) of giving harbor
to the God-defying refugees from the just displeasure of offended
Massachusetts, were selected as the first victims of the series.

The United Colonies, accordingly, entered into a league with
Uncas, as chief sachem of the Mohegans (though there is reason to
believe that only their patronage made him so), under which they
they encouraged him to perpetrate annoyances and encroachments
on the Narragansetts, denying them, at the same time, any resort
to their traditional methods of redress ; and whenever any complaint was made to them by either Uncas or Miantonomi or any
adherent of either, their decision was, invariably, adverse to the
Narragansett, and he was enjoined to good behaviour on pain of
punishment and the displeasure of the United Colonies, they being
the allies and friends of Uncas, as they constantly took occasion to
promulgate.   Any person who will examine the records of the
Commissioners of the United Colonies impartially will endorse the
accuracy of this statement ; the instances are too numerous for
quotation or even for special reference.

The fruits of this policy were very soon apparent, the Narragansetts, denied justice by the English and prohibited from any
retribution on the Mohegans for wrongs suffered from them, according to their traditional customs, were provoked into such acts
toward the Mohegans as made them amenable to English ideas of
justice, and afforded the pretexts which the English sought.   The
United Colonies accordingly, despite the remonstrances of Roger
Williams, who knew all the parties and appreciated the truthful

and manly character of the Narragansett chief and the wily and treacherous disposition of Uncas, united with the Mohegans in a war on the Narragansetts, which culminated in the prostration of the Narragansett power and the capture of Miantonomi.

After the mockery of a trial by the English, at Hartford, Miantonomi was given up to Uncas for execution, and the Narragansett tribe was fined 2000 fathoms of peague, an amount utterly beyond their ability to pay. This levy was founded (as I have said before) on the pretext, principle, if it please you, so to express it, of. making the conquered pay the expenses of all parties.

To enable the Indians to pay this excessive mulct, after their resources had been drained by the war, the principal men of the conquering party, to wit, John Winthrop, Governor of Connecticut, Major Humphrey Atherton, Richard Smith, Richard Smith, junior, Lieutenant William Hudson of Boston, Ambrose Dickenson of Boston, and John Ticknor of Nashaway (no doubt out of their great generosity toward the poor natives) formed themselves into what we should call a "Credit Mobilier," though they, probably, had never heard that phrase, advanced the sum required and received therefor deeds of the tracts of land known ever after as the Atherton purchases. One of these was a mortgage, of course never redeemed.

Nothing can better illustrate the typical thrift of the Yankee character than the settlement of these conquests.

Firstly, having used the Narragansetts and Mohegans as a scourge to the Pequots, our pious friends of the United Colonies appropriate their lands and then tax their allies for the services of the remnant whom they have given them as slaves.

Secondly, with the help of the Mohegans, they whip the Narragansetts and impose a fine which involves the forfeiture of their lands, and the Mohegans whistle for their share in the division.

Thirdly, the Mohegans having been made instrumental in destroying the other tribes, who might, and probably would, at a future time, have made common cause with them, they are wiped out at the pleasure of their patrons, when their possessions are more available than their services.

One is reminded of the old story, in which the white hunter says to the Indian, "You take the buzzard and I'll take the turkey, or I'll take the turkey and you take the buzzard."

In this transaction originated those titles which occasioned so much dispute during the remainder of the seventeenth century, and also the claim of jurisdiction on the part of Connecticut. Volumes might be filled with the correspondence and acts of the colonies, and of the Commissioners of the United Colonies, and of the various Royal Commissioners, and of other commissions, and in all these, conflicting and confusing as they are to the last degree, the name of John Greene perpetually appears as the undeviating champion of the rights of Rhode Island colony, and of Rhode Island proprietorship.

On the third of February, 1678-9, answer is made by Randall Holden and John Greene (then in London) to some questions by the Lords of Trade and Plantations relative to Mount Hope, and in an order of the King in council, of date 12th same month, they are mentioned as our well beloved subjects R. Holden and J. Greene, and in consequence of their representations of the facts in the case, and as to their personal knowledge of the submission of the sachem and chiefs to the King's government, April 19, 1644, and that their submission had been accepted by the Royal Commissioners : the order then reiterates, that the pretended purchase by Major Atherton and others of the Massachusetts Bay had been declared void, and the purchasers had been ordered to vacate the lands, and the authorities of Rhode Island to exercise jurisdiction over them. Taking the premises into consideration, the King orders that matters remain as they now are until further orders, and directs that a copy be sent to Massachusetts, Plymouth and Connecticut. [R. I. Col. Rec., vol. 3, p. 40-1.]

On the third of July, 1678, on the petition of Richard Smith, John Winthrop, Josiah Winslow, William Harris, John Viall and

10

others, the King in council orders that the matter be referred to the Board of Trade and Plantations. The decision of this was confirmatory of the other. December 13, 1678.

July 29, 1679, another petition, of similar import, is replied to by Randall Holden and John Greene.

September 17, 1683, an appeal is made by Randall Holden and John Greene, on the part of the inhabitants of Warwick and the citizens of Rhode Island, on the occasion of Governor Cranfield's Court, held at Richard Smith's house in Narragansett, which the government of Rhode Island declined to recognize, on the ground that they refused to show their commission.

As seven of the nine commissioners, in fact all but one of those who formed the Court, were citizens of Massachusetts or Connecticut, and several of them claimants to land, under the Atherton purchases, selected, no doubt, by Governor Cranfield and Edward Randolph, both violent partizans and palpably inimical to Rhode Island; it is not to be wondered at that they chose any course rather than plead before such a tribunal.

As was expected, Governor Cranfield's commission made a report recommending the vesting the government in Connecticut, and confirming Major Atherton and his associates in the proprietorship. This is dated October 20, 1683. [R. I. Col. Rec., vol. 3, p. 137-49.]

Edward Cranfield, Lieutenant Governor of New Hampshire, William Stoughton, Joseph Dudley, Edward Randolph, Samuel Shrimpton, John Fitz Winthrop, Edward Palmer, John Pyncheon and Nathaniel Saltonstall, were the commissioners appointed by Charles II, 1683, 35th year of reign.

The request of the Assembly sitting at Warwick to see the commission under which they acted, was presented to the commissioners sitting at Richard Smith's house at Narragansett, August 21, 1683, by Captain James Greene and William Allin. Next day answer was returned, through the same messengers, by Governor Cranfield, that he knew no Governor in King's Province. The same

day, the Assembly, now sitting at Captain John Fones' house (" to
be near the Court of Commissioners "), in view of the facts, direct
the Governor and Council to prohibit the Court, "and to require
all persons t) depart peaceably, on pain of contempt of the King's
authority." This prohibition recites that the Governor and Council " being bound, by virtue of His Majesty's commission, under
the Great Seal, &c., to provide for the peace and safety of His
Majesty's subjects here, do, in His Majesty's name, prohibit the
said Edward Cranfield and his associates for keeping Court in any
part of this jurisdiction, and we do also hereby require, in His
Majesty's name, every person or persons within the verge of this
colony and King's Province, peaceably to depart, and not be abet-
tors to the said pretended Court, on pain of contempt of His Majesty's authority." Signed,

WILLIAM CODDINGTON, Governor (the younger).

WALTER CLARKE, Deputy Governor.

JOHN EASTON, Assistant.

ARTHUR FENNER, "

JOSEPH JENCKES, "

RICHARD ARNOLD, "

JOHN ALBRO, "

GEORGE LAWTON, "

JOHN GREENE, "

BENJAMIN BARTON, "

August 24, 1683, in answer to a letter from Governor Cranfield, saying that by their neglect and contempt of His Majesty's
commission he was necessitated to adjourn to Boston, they say :—

"Whereunto we answer, that we are heartily sorry that you
should, through your unneighborly deportment in this government,
withhold from us the sight of your commission, so to contemn His
Majesty's authority here as to hinder us from being serviceable to
His Majesty therein. And for your slighting His Majesty's authority here, have extorted from us a prohibition against your further proceeds ; notwithstanding we had used all our endeavors,

by transporting our records and holding, adjourning and continu-
ing His Majesty's General Court here four days time and upwards,
in hopes and expectation of your compliance, that we might have
served His Majesty herein, as formerly we have done, and have to
show His Majesty's gracious letters in approbation thereof." [R.
I. Col. Rec., vol. 3, p. 128-32.]

> Your neighbors and friends,
>
> JOHN POTTER, Clerk.
>
> By order of the Court.

In a letter dated Sept. 15, 1683, the Assembly send their ver-
sion of this transaction, and intimate their claim to an appeal from
any adverse decision.

On Sept. 17, 1683, Randall Holden and John Greene present an
address to the King, reiterating their statement made in 1678-9,
which, at that time, procured a decision favorable to their claims.
[For these two, see R. I. Col. Rec. vol. 3, p. 135-8.]

In Gov. Cranfield's account of proceedings, to Board of Trade
and Plantations, he says :—

"Accordingly, all appeared except the Rhode Islanders, who,
the same day of our convention, did assemble their General Court,
and sent one Captain Greene, with a letter from them, to prohibit
our proceedings.

" They are a people utterly incapable of managing a government ; these inclosed will sufficiently evidence their injustice and
maladministration. The agents that they formerly employed, were
Captains Holden and Greene, where, in a petition to His Majesty,
they set forth that the occasion of their troubles befel them because
of the consonancy of their judgments to the Church of England,
who are well known to be far from it.

" As to the purchase they made of the Indian kings, for all the
land of Rhode Island and Providence and thereabouts, was only
during the life of William Coddington and his friends; there being
but two living now that now that can be called his friends, the
purchase being not made in the name of the government and their

successors must devolve upon His Majesty."—with many other very disparaging remarks. [R. I Col. Rec., vol. 3, p. 146.]

Governor Coddington also writes a letter of explanation to the King. [R I. Col. Rec., vol. 3, p. 147-9.]

An address from the Justices of the Peace of the Narragansett country to the King, dated 1686, probably under Secretary Randolph and President Dudley, preceding the arrival of Governor Andros, contains the following passages :—

"Most humbly sheweth, that the plantation and settlement of your Majesty's said province, having been long interrupted and discouraged by the pretensions and power of the government of Rhode Island, and more especially, as your petitioners are informed, by the ill designs and practices of Major John Greene of Warwick, a person of a restless and turbulent spirit, and others his accomplices, in the colony of Rhode Island, who, by misrepresentations to His late Majesty's commissioners and false suggestions to His late Majesty in council, and by the exhibition of false deeds and informations on several occasions, have not only greatly disquieted your Majesty's subjects in said province, and hindered, what in them lies, the further settlement of the same, but also oppressed their neighbors of Pawtuxet in the said colony of Rhode Island.

" And your petitioners, being informed by good evidence that upon the late establishment of your Royal government here, and the publication thereof by the President and council (i. e., after the suspension of the charter), the said Major Greene, with James Greene his brother, and others of the town of Warwick, in great contempt of your Majesty's gracious authority and government, tore down, from a public place in this your province, and carried away the proclamation of your Majesty's gracious pleasure and care for the government of your subjects here, and hath since refused the mediation of your Majesty's President and Governor of Rhode Island, and all other just and regular ways and means for settlement of boundaries of said town of Warwick, and quieting the contentions and disputes which said Greene, by false deeds and other

11

ill means, hath stirred up and maintained against your Majesty's
subjects here, and we, your Majesty's petitioners, being further informed that the said Major Greene with others, intend contriving
to retard the regulations your Majesty hath thought so greatly
needful for that colony of Rhode Island and Providence Plantations, and to disturb the peace and progress of this plantation,
hath, in a secret manner and upon many misrepresentations, drawn
sundry of the inhabitants of Rhode Island to subscribe such papers
as he, to that end, hath prepared: and to contribute money to
maintain and carry on his causeless complaints at your Royal Court,
to which he is now gone, having no lawful power from the Governor and company of Rhode Island so to do.

"Your petitioners most humbly pray, that as your Majesty has
most graciously manifested your care for the peace and prosperity
of this poor plantation, in annexing the same to the government of
of Massachusetts; so that your Majesty would still continue your
just and tender regard thereto, and give check to the ill designs
of the said Major Greene and others, pretending power from Rhode
Island and Providence Plantations, and that you would graciously
refer the same to the examination and determination of your general Governor and council here, or other competent judges, where
all your Majesty's subjects concerned may have opportunity to be
heard.

"And your petitioners, as in duty bound, shall ever pray."
Signed by the Justices of King's Province.
New England, 1686.   [R. I. Col. Rec., vol. 3, p. 208-9.]

On the same page [R. I. Col. Rec.] is an application, to the
same effect, from Nathaniel Thomas, attorney to some proprietors
of Pawtuxet, viz., That the King would refer their case to the Governor (Andros) and council of New England.

These men, subscribers to this petition, were some of them
Major Atherton's partners in the purchase (which one or more of
the King's orders defines as pretended purchase) and all of them
held under it; their expressions shew that they belonged to the

kon-

~~now~~ popular party, particularly that which demonstrates their satisfaction at being placed under Massachusetts. This was the fulfilment of their long cherished desire. President Dudley also was a member of the Cranfield commission. But the chief point I intended to make, in introducing it, is the emphatic and conclusive testimony it affords to the faithfulness and energy with which John Greene, and other people of Warwick, sustained and defended the rights and interests of Rhode Island, and his paramount importance in this controversy.

As Governor Cranfield's commission effected no result, and as the Rhode Island colony subsisted and flourished for nearly one hundred years after, and as the same community has carried on the government, with some degree of success, to this day, we may well afford to forbear comment on his assertion, that "they are a people incapable of managing a government." But I will not hesitate to say, that their success in this matter, considering all the powerful influences they encountered, is a triumphant vindication of their courage, their capacity and their executive ability.

I have made these extracts from the very voluminous records in relation to the Narragansett controversy, to show the active and persistent efforts made by John Greene in behalf of Rhode Island claims to a tract of territory on which, without doubt, depended her existence, without intending to elucidate the obscurities of it. As regards them we may be satisfied with the consummation, which was, the settlement of proprietary claims by compromise, and the assignment of the jurisdiction to Rhode Island.

The partizan character of the Cranfield commission is palpable from its holding its session at the house of Richard Smith, one of the Atherton purchasers and a loud-mouthed adherent of Connecticut, and from the whole tenor of its acts.

The final settlement recognized the sales under the Atherton purchase, not because of its validity, but because the occupants had purchased in good faith, and to disturb them in its occupancy and to deprive them of their improvements and of the homes which many years of labour had reclaimed from the wilderness, would have been unjust as well as inexpedient.

The strength of the position taken by the commission, consisting of Sir Robert Carr, George Cartwright and Samuel Maverick, in their report dated March 29, 1664, in relation to Atherton purchases, " that the said country having been granted to His Majesty, all such Indian titles are void," is irrefragable, and it appears to me that the whole transaction, as between the United Colonies and the Narragansett tribe, was as unjustifiable in law as if one county in England should make war on another, and confiscate their lands to idemnify the invaders for the expenses they had incurred in prosecuting the enterprise, and equally a violation of His Majesty's peace.

A writ of quo warranto was issued, on the application of Edward Randolph, dated Oct. 6, 1685, and was received in Rhode Island June 22, 1686. June 29th same month, the Assembly voted that they would not contest the suit, but would, by humble address, ask His Majesty, " To continue our privileges and liberties, according to our charter, formerly granted by his late Majesty Charles the Second, of blessed memory.

During the administration of Sir Edmond Andros the name of John Greene does not appear on the record. He appears as one of those named of the council, but he, probably, never took the engagement, and as the Narragansett petitioners say, sometime in 1686 he was about going to England, probably he was absent a part of that time. But at the first session after Andros' downfall, Feb. 26, 1689-90, he was present in the Assembly as assistant and acted as clerk.

He was also one of the signers of the address to their Majesties King William and Queen Mary, Jan. 30, 1689-90.

In May 1690, John Easton was elected Governor and John Greene Lieutenant Governor.

In Sir Edmond Andros' account of his administration and imprisonment he makes no complaint of Rhode Island people, and therefore we may conclude they submitted quietly, although they must have been restive under a condition so foreign to their habits and so contrary to their sentiments.

In 1696 a controversy began, during which the name of John Greene was subjected to some aspersions which, I think, were unmerited.

It appears that, previously to this time, the colonists had taken it for granted that the charter gave them admiralty powers, and they had commissioned vessels as privateers, and their courts had adjudicated upon prizes, "et id omne genus," and it is obvious that, had they not so done, they would have been, in case of war, at the mercy of any maratime enemy. There, had, until now, no trade existed of sufficient magnitude to induce the establishment of custom houses and courts of admiralty on our thinly peopled coasts. No royal ships were stationed at the mouths of our harbors, no strong forts bristling with artillery were erected, as now, on the headlands that commanded them, to defend them from predatory incursions. Consequently, the authorities were only too glad to encourage such adventurous spirits as were willing to take the risk, to fit out armed vessels to annoy and damage the King's enemies on the high seas. It appears also, that some of those commissions were signed by John Greene as Lieutenant Governor.

Now I don't make any pretensions to legal knowledge, and can't presume to determine the legality of such commissions, but, it appears to me if they were not legal they were void. As there is no evidence to the contrary, or assertion even, I conclude that captures were made and prizes condemned under them, and nothing was said about their questionable character until 1697, when the war closed ; then it was charged, that some of these vessels had been engaged in piracies in the Indian ocean. Now there is nothing to sustain this that would, for a moment, pass as evidence, although it would not be very improbable that men such as usually compose a privateer's company, after living in that manner for some years, on the accession of peace, should, like the free companions of Europe, resort to such courses.

12

Now let us look into such evidence as we have.

February 9, 1696-7, in a letter from the Board of Trade to the Governor and company of Rhode Island [See R. I. Col. Rec., vol. 3, p. 322] they say, " We are obliged, in giving you this notice to recommend it, so much the more particularly to your care, by reason that upon occasion of the late trials, of some of Avery's crew here, several informations have been transmitted to us, wherein mention is made of Rhode Island as a place where pirates are, ordinarily, too kindly entertained." Some of the expressions in those papers are as follows :—

" William Mews, a pirate, fitted out at Rhode Island. Thomas Jones is concerned in the old bark with Captain Want, and lives in Rhode Island. Want is gone into the Gulf of Persia, and in all probability is at Rhode Island or Carolina by this time. Want's wife lives there. Want broke up there about three years ago, after a good voyage, and spent his money there and in Pennsylvania."

In answer to this Governor Cranston writes, after quoting the section above :—

[R. I. Col. Rec., vol. 3, p. 337.] "Whereunto we humbly answer, that things are misrepresented to His Majesty and your lordships, and that this, His Majesty's government, was never concerned in or countenanced such things. And we are certain that William Mayes had his clearance from the custom house here, to go on a trading voyage to Madagascar, with a lawful commission to fight the French, His Majesty's enemies, from the government; and the best information we can have is, that Captain Avery and his men plundered him ; and we very much suspect that they have destroyed him and his company, for none of them are yet returned, or any news of any one particular person belonging to said Mayes. And as for Captain Want, we neither know the man or ever had a sight of his ship, William Mayes being all the person that ever was commissionated from this government, that has been to the southward of the Cape of Good Hope.

" Furthermore, we have seized two persons and their moneys,

who came into (our) authority, one Robert Munday and George
Cutler, who, upon examination, do deny that they have been any
further than Madagascar : but we shall endeavor to search out the
truth and bring them to trial."

In answer to a letter from Lord Shrewsbury, dated Sept. 25,
1697, the Assembly issued a proclamation, dated May 4, 1698, requiring all magistrates to bring to justice, and all citizens to aid in
convicting, any person suspected of piracy, &c. [R. I. Col. Rec.,
vol. 3, p. 338.]

May 30, 1698, Elward Randolph writes to the Board of Trade.
[R. I. Col. Rec., vol. 3, p. 339-40.] He says :—

The management of the government (such as it is) is in the
hands of Quakers and Anabaptists. Neither judges, juries nor
witnesses are under any obligation, so that all things are managed
there according to their will and interest.

"Mr. Brenton delivered the commissions to the several officers
of the Court of Admiralty, to be erected in that colony, which Mr.
Clarke, the late Governor, objected to.

"Colonel Peleg Sanford, judge of the said court, went to
Walter Clarke, when he was Governor, to be sworn to the true
performance of his office, Clarke took his commission from him,
carried it to the Assembly, sitting about that time, and acquainted
them that the allowing of a Court of Admiralty in this colony
would utterly destroy their charter, by which they were empowered
to erect a Court of Admiralty, and appoint the officers thereunto
belonging.

"Sometime after, Colonel Sanford demanded his commission
(for judge) of Walter Clarke, which he then absolutely refused to
give him.

"The present Governor has likewise refused to give the judge
of the Court of Admiralty his oath, telling me that he has no
authority or directions for so doing.

"Not long before my landing at Rhode Island, eight pirates
came from Fisher's Island (belonging to the present Governor of

Connecticut colony), with a great deal of money and East India commodities, which they brought in their brigantine (from Madagascar), now lying in New York.

" Upon the arrival of the Fawn frigate in Rhode Island harbor, six men made their escape from thence to Boston, with a great quantity of East India goods and money, but Robert Munday and George Cutler (two of them) were seized upon, and about £1,400 or £1,500 in silver and gold was taken from them, and (as the Governor tells me) is in his custody. They were put in prison, but about two days after, they were admitted to bail by the Governor's order (as I am informed), Gresham [perhaps Latham] Clarke, one of the Governor's uncles, being their security; by which means, they have an opportunity given to escape, leaving their money to be shared by the Governor and his two uncles, who have been very great gainers by the pirates which have frequented Rhode Island. Three or four vessels have been fitted out from thence, to the Red Sea.

" Walter Clarke, the late Governor, and his brother, now the recorder of the place, have countenanced pirates, and enriched themselves thereby, their Deputy Governor, John Greene, granted a commission to one of the pirates (who went from thence to the Red Sea), without any security given by the master.

" There are a great many men in Rhode Island groaning under this lawless government, who would do His Majesty faithful service if either put under His Majesty's immediate government or annexed to the province of Massachusetts Bay. They have offered to allow £500 per annum towards the support of a person appointed by His Majesty over them. Till that's done, 'tis not possible for the Earl of Bellomont to suppress illegal trade and piracy, which were, most notoriously, countenanced and supported in this place, and to this day continued in Rhode Island colony.

" P. S. June 6. I am this day informed that the Governor of Rhode Island intends to appoint a court to proceed to the trial of Munday and Cutler, the pirates whose money the Governor has in his hands, and in case nobody appears (to prosecute them for piracy), to acquit them and deliver them their money, notwithstanding the Earl of Bellomont sent them His Majesty's circular letter, directed to all Governors in the plantations, to seize and apprehend the ships, goods and effects of all persons suspected for piracy, &c., which, as I remember, Governor Cranston acknowledged to some he had received."

Here is a picture presented of a conspiracy on the part of the officials of a government (which in the same paper is denounced as being in the hands of Quakers and Anabaptists, ("God save the mark") as in fact it was chiefly, in complicity with John Greene, whom we have no reason to to believe to have been either a Quaker or a Baptist, to prey upon maratime property, through the instrumentality of agents like Captain Kidd and his less famous congeners. Imagine Walter Clarke, who refused to take an oath, saying (as Mr. Randolph says) that he always spoke "as in the presence of God," and Latham Clarke, one of the earliest and most zealous disciples of George Fox, and Governor Cranston, their nephew, who, unfortunately for Mr. Randolph, belonged to the establishment and was one of the founders and earnest friends of Trinity Church, Newport—imagine these, the sons and grandson of Jeremiah Clarke the refugee, first from England, and then from Massachusetts "for conscience sake," and on the other hand their brother, James Clarke, pastor of the Second Baptist Church, and John Clarke, pastor of the First Baptist Church, and Chad Brown and Pardon Tillinghast, laying plans for robbery on the high seas, while Roger Williams and George Fox look on and smile approval! Is there anything absurd in such a picture? And yet, you must entertain just such a picture if you give a particle of credence to Mr. Randolph's story. Still, Mr. Randolph may have been sincere in believing it himself. He came to America to subserve the purposes of the crown, according to the mistaken views of the crown's interests then prevailing : to restrain the people in their privileges, to cut off, as much as possible, their liberties, of which he honestly

13

believed them unworthy, and of whose proper enjoyment he judged
them incapable. He came to aid in establishing the machinery
which would give the crown the largest revenue, and its hungry
adherents the fattest pickings, which should restrain the colonists
of any trade that might compete with home merchants, which should
absolutely prohibit the inauguration of any industry that might
furnish the colonists with any commodity that the mother country
could hope to furnish at a profit, in fine, he came to initiate that
system which finally drove the colonies to successful resistance.
He did nothing but what was perfectly natural, no more and no
less than his duty, when he allied himself with the party which proposed, through him, to dispense with their franchises, to place themselves under a personal government, administered either by himself or some other minion of courtly favor, or to throw themselves
at the feet of the royal government, and become an integral part of
Massachusetts, their ancient and relentless enemy.

We may here pause, and dwell somewhat on the enormity of
this proposition and its possible consequences. It proposes to ab-
dicate and dissolve the glorious old charter of 1663 : the charter
which gave the first example in the history of man, of freedom of
thought secured by royal recognition, which gave to the toil-worn
colonists a hope of fruition from the struggles and sufferings of
their earlier years, and which, toward the end of their career, seemed
to promise to their posterity security for the enjoyment of those
fruits—the charter which, for nearly two hundred years, not only
procured safety, prosperity and comparative happiness to those who
lived under it, but furnished a model for a great proportion of more
modern free states—the charter for which Roger Williams and John
Clarke and Randall Holden and John Greene had striven many
years, "through good report and through evil report"—the charter
around which the affections of Rhode Islanders had so entwined
themselves, that when its final struggle for existence came, it was
yielded up on the decree of inexorable fate, and only on compul-
sion, and not without many bitter pangs to the bereft, although its

want of adaptation to the times was apparent, and although, for many years, it had been only the shadow of its former self. It had been nursed in its decrepitude for seventy years as a virtuous off-spring nurses a decrepit parent, though the royal franchises, which it represented, had long inhered in themselves of their own proper and sovereign right. And this these men proposed, that they might, for a short time, "bask in the sunshine of royal favor," and indulge their rancor in the mortification of their opponents, regardless alike of the well being of posterity and of the public good. How far the accomplishment of their design might have retarded the advancement of mankind it would be presumptuous to conjecture, but it is not too much to say that at this time Rhode Island was the battleground on which the conflict of ideas was prosecuted with most earnestness, and her collapse may have thrown the hands far back on the dial of time, Massachusetts having already succumbed. She had a Governor of royal appointment from 1686 to 1776.

That Governor Clarke and Governor Cranston, believing it an infringement of their chartered rights, refused to recognize the commissions of Mr. Peleg Sanford as judge, and of Mr. Nathaniel Coddington as clerk, in admiralty, is very much to their credit from our point of view, thought not likely to be so regarded at court.

The story in relation to pirates, possibly has some groundwork, but, under any view, sustains no charge against anybody of criminal design ; there might be good reasons for suspicion without possibility of arriving at adequate proof. If a failure to convict criminals is to be always construed as a proof of complicity on the part of government, where would all modern governments find themselves ? These stories of Mr. Randolph's are all founded on hearsay, and assumption of guilt on the part of all parties implicated. You would not hang a dog on any such evidence ; will you then give any weight to it, in estimating men to whose services you owe so much, and whose whole lives condemn the testimony.

The rest of the documents relating to this subject [to be found in R. I. Col. Rec. for 1697-9] are of the same character, they were never the subject of any judicial investigation ; only those from the Board of Trade could have been seen by any contemporaries, and they only by very few on this side of the water, and none of them were ever expected to see the light again, buried as they were in the vortex of the British Colonial Office, nor would they but for the indomitable industry of our worthy president, Governor Arnold, and the patriotic munificence of our late fellow-citizen, John Carter Brown. We only get, however, one side of the case ; it is pretty difficult to get in the defence if the plaintiff does not prosecute In this case the plaintiffs had no such design, their intention was to affect the ear of administration, through Mr. Randolph and Lord Bellomont, with as little opportunity as possible for replication.

The plaintiff in this case, is the party against which the colony has been struggling from its inception ; the same party, whose in-itial steps were taken at Pawtuxet in 1643; the same party which, headed by Coddington and Partridge attempted to divorce Rhode Island from Providence and Warwick, in 1648, which, ignoring them, asked that the island be taken under the guardianship of the United Colonies ; the same party with whom John Greene entered the lists in his early youth, and with whom he wrestled out his long life for the integrity of our own territory and for the preser-vation of King's county from Connecticut, and for the great prin-ciple of civil liberty.

This party was willing, nay, anxious (as Randolph's letter proves), to have the charter abrogated and Rhode Island annexed to Massachusetts, both to be under a Governor and Council, of royal appointment, or otherwise deprived of her comparative inde-pendence. This obsequious spirit now showing itself so distinct-ly at the close of the seventeenth century, was preserved and nursed by the same party, though numerically small, until it cul-minated in the toryism of the Revolution. This division of parties became almost a birthright, and the same families are represented throughout the whole interval, from 1643 to 1783, on opposite sides. No variation appears on the part of any of the Greenes of Warwick from their fealty to popular rights and Rhode Island interests.

In some of the papers I have referred to, the charges of Mr. Randolph are reiterated and supported by Messrs. Sanford, Coddington, &c., but nothing appears, amounting to proof, sufficient to justify suspicion of complicity on the part of Governor Cranston, or of any of the Clarkes, or of John Greene.

In the report of Lord Bellomont to the Board of Trade, Nov. 27, 1699, he says:—

[R. I. Col. Rec., vol. 3, p. 387.] "John Greene, a brutish man, of very corrupt or no principles in religion, and generally known so to be by the people, is notwithstanding, from year to year, anew elected and continued in the place of Deputy Governor and second magistrate of the colony; whilst several gentlemen, most sufficient for estate, are neglected, and no ways employed in any office or place in the government, but on the contrary maligned for their good affection to His Majesty's service.

"The aforesaid Deputy Governor Greene, during the time of the late war, granted several sea commissions, under the public seal of the colony, unto private men of war (otherwise pirates), expressly contrary to the will of the Governor, then in the actual exercise of the government; and notwithstanding his forbidding the same, took no security of the persons to whom the same were granted, nor could he tell, by the contents of them, who was to execute the same, being directed, in an unusual manner, to the Captain, his assignee or assignees, and otherwise full of tautologies and nonsense. And all the vessels, whereof the commanders were so commissionated, went to Madagascar and the seas of India, and were employed to commit piracy. The said Greene is likewise complained of for exercising divers other exorbitant and arbitrary acts of power, under color of his office."

John Easton, senior, makes a declaration, June 4, 1698, to this effect:—

14

[R. I. Col. Rec., vol. 3, p. 340-1.] "I, John Easton, senior, who was, by the people, elected and chosen to the place of Governor of His Majesty's colony of Rhode Island and Providence Plantations, in America, in the year 1694, do declare, that Whereas John Greene, living in the town of Warwick, was Deputy Governor for the colony, in said year did give forth a commission to John Banks, · a privateer, one who was come into Newport, with one Captain Thomas Tew, a privateer: this may certify, that I would not give any commission to said Banks nor any other, to go out on any such designs they went upon, wherefore he got a commission from said Greene, who without my order or privity did give said Banks a commission, though I did use what means I could to prevent the same.

"And furthermore, I never was against giving any commission to any, that might be for the security of the King's interests in this colony, and that there may not things be otherways resented against us than they were, I have and do declare as abovesaid."

Attested by Nathaniel Coddington, Assistant.

Thus I have presented the whole case against John Greene. Lord Bellomont says "he is a very brutish man;" this, as we do not know that his lordship ever saw him (and, as his duties lay in Massachusetts, he probably never did), may pass for what it is worth; it would be difficult to gainsay at this time of day.. His religious principles, probably, his lordship judges by the high church standard of that day—the same standard by which Mr. Randolph is governed, in denouncing Quakers and Baptists as unworthy of confidence. It was perhaps for the reason of his brutishness that John Greene was several times selected to represent the colony at the Court of London, and as he was preeminently successful in all these missions, a very low degree of refinement must be argued in relation to the Court.

Lord Bellomont repeats Mr. Randolph's hint that there are several gentlemen of estate, well affected to His Majesty, who would be willing to fill the places of these inferior persons, whom the people constantly prefer. This, to the average mind, only argues that the people understood who were their friends, and preferred to entrust their interests to them, rather than to the friends of somebody else.

His lordship charges that Greene granted several commissions to private men of war (otherwise pirates). Now Governor Cranston says, explicitly, that only one vessel with a commission from Rhode Island ever went to the eastward (or as he says, southward) of Cape Good Hope, and he, certainly, may be supposed to know whereof he speaks. You shall judge for yourselves whose testimony is worth the most: Lord Bellomont, Royal Governor of Massachusetts, who may or may not have been in Rhode Island in his life, and all whose statements are loose and not nearer than third-hand, and who had axes to grind for himself and his friends, and the interest of patrons to subserve; or Governor Cranston, who was for thirty successive years Governor of the colony, by popular choice. We know the character of our ancestors too well to believe any impeachment of a man so honored with their confidence.

The entire collapse of their schemes, and their utter failure in accomplishing the ends they sought, is the sufficient refutation of all these slanders.

The only point remaining is the affidavit of Governor Easton. This, I confess, is an extraordinary document, and the only explanation possible is that he was his dotage. I don't mean to claim that John Greene was, although then, 1694, seventy-five years of age; Governor Easton being, at the date of his statement, seventy-seven or eight.

That a man who was Governor, and who lived in the port whence a vessel sailed, should not have it in his power, if so disposed, to prevent her going to sea, without proper papers or with improper ones, is incomprehensible. That John Greene, or anybody else, should imagine that he could give a commission of any validity against the will of the Governor, and in fact without his express authority, is equally incomprehensible. The only ex-

planation of the fact that the issue of privateers' commissions was
entrusted to the Deputy Governor is, that Governor Easton, Governor Caleb Carr and Governor Walter Clarke, who were in office
from 1693 to 1697, or during the war, were all Quakers and had
scruples about signing warlike commissions.

Attached to Governor Easton's statement is this, not signed
by him :—

"And the abovesaid, John Easton, did declare to me, the day
abovesaid, that in the abovsaid year (1694), Captain Thomas Tew
came to him and proffered him £500 if he would give him a commission ; to which he answered he knew not his design, and the
said Tew replyed he should go where, perhaps, the commission
might never be seen or heard of, the which he wholly refused to
give, and further saith not.   Taken before me,

NATHANIEL CODDINGTON, Assistant."

This, as evidence against John Greene, has three vital defects.
First, it does not charge, much less prove, that Captain Tew was a
pirate : second, it does not even intimate that he was commissioned
by John Greene ; third, it does not say that he received any commission at all.

Recollect, that Nathaniel Coddington was to be clerk in admiralty in the proposed court of which Peleg Sanford was to be judge,
and see whether this does not bear the marks of a little sharp practice on the part of those gentlemen. This was never to be exposed,
never to be refuted.   The logic of this argument is of the same
order as that of the luminous individual who "did not wonder they
called it Stony Stratford, 'twas so infested with fleas."

There can be no doubt that whatever was done by John Greene
was done in good faith ; it was not the first instance nor the last,
of the abuse of privateers' commissions, supposing there were any
grounds for any of the stories.   Probably, if the truth were known,
there have, ere now, pirates sailed out of the ports of Great Britain
itself, with a commission bearing the sign-manual of the King, and
with a big disc of beeswax, emblazoned with the royal arms, affixed

or suffixed ; but the occasion was too opportune to be neglected by the high prerogative royalists of the opposite party.

We should bear in mind that these transactions are not to be judged in the light of our days; only about one hundred years before, the Queen of England had fitted out fleets for piratical purposes, and Drake and Hawkins had received ovations from the English people for the successful prosecution of them ; that the intervening period was a very disturbed one ; that maritime law had not, as now, become a science : that Mr. Randolph and Lord Bellomont by no means charged Rhode Island with a monopoly of irregularities, all the other colonies being equally the subjects of censure. Indeed no vessel could go to sea unless fully armed and manned, and as a matter of course all owners of vessels desired, and usually obtained, an offensive commission in all times of war, so as to offset contingent prize money against absolute risk. Therefore the sea swarmed with armed vessels, it being a general maritime war. No wonder many of these became pirates, not improbably some of those with Rhode Island commissions.

I do not imagine that John Greene had legal attainments rivalling those of Sir Edward Coke ; he should have had to enable him to encounter the able adversaries of his earlier career, but especially to have escaped the animadversions of the royal agents, whose mission was to find flaws in colonial armour. The manner of issuing commissions was probably identical with that which had been usual in Rhode Island, as also in the other colonies, and possibly not as artistic as those issued from London.

I finish with John Greene, by expressing the belief that no name is better entitled than his to the respect and gratitude of every true Rhode Islander.

Of the sons of John Greene

John, the eldest, died young.

Peter, appears several times as deputy from Warwick.

Job, Freeman, May 1681, frequently deputy from Warwick,
several times assistant, was grandfather of Colonel

15

Christopher Greene; his daughter Deborah was the
second wife of Simon Ray, and mother of Mrs. Governor Samuel Ward and of Mrs. Governor William
Greene, 2d., and grandmother of Mrs. General Nathaniel Greene.

Philip, does not appear in the public record.

Richard, Freeman, May 1685, deputy 1699 to 1704, assistant
1704 to 1711, when he died, and his brother Job was
elected to the vacancy.

SAMUEL GREENE.

Samuel, youngest son of John Greene, 2d., and father of the first Governor William Greene, was deputy in 1704, 7, 8, 14, 15 and 19. He seems to have been less active in colonial affairs than some of his brothers. He was a very substantial kind of man and highly respected. He was distinguished for his extraordinary stature, for which the family were remarkable. He died in 1720, aged 50 years.

The children of Samuel Greene were,

William (Governor), born March 16, 1695, died February 1758, married Catharine Greene of Benjamin (Tobacco Ben), May 22, 1720.

Mary, born August 25, 1698, married Thomas Fry.

Samuel, born October 23, 1700, married Sarah Coggeshall of Joshua.

Benjamin, born January 5, 1702-3, married Mary Angell of Samuel.

Anne, born April 5, 1706, died June 30, 1706.

FIRST GOVERNOR WILLIAM GREENE.

William Greene, son of Samuel, 2d., of John, 2d., of John, 1st., was born March 16, 1695-6, and died February 1758, aged 62 years. His wife was Catharine Greene, daughter of Benjamin, 3d., of Thomas, 2d., of John, 1st. The wife of Thomas, 2d., was Elizabeth Barton of Rufus, so that the children of this marriage unite two streams from the blood of 1st John Greene to one from Barton, and also, by other marriages, one from Holden, Gorton and Carder.

Governor Greene's brother Samuel married Sarah Coggeshall of Joshua, and was ancestor of William Greene Williams, esquire, of Providence, who also has the honor to represent Roger Williams in the direct line.

His sister Mary was the wife of Thomas Fry, who was Deputy Governor from 1727 to 1729, and was ancestor of Hon. Alfred Anthony of Providence.

He had also a brother Benjamin, who married Mary Angell of Samuel.

Governor Greene's children were,

Benjamin, born May 19, 1724; his son, Colonel William Greene of Warwick neck, married Celia, daughter of his brother Governor William, and has numerous descendants well known in Providence.

Samuel, born August 25, 1727, married Patience Cooke, of Benjamin and was ancestor of Hon. Samuel G. Arnold.

William, (future Governor,) born August 16, 1731, died November 29, 1809.

Margaret, born November 2, 1733, married Rufus Spencer, 2d wife.

Catharine, born December 9, 1735, married John Greene of Boston.

Christopher, born April 18, 1741, died same year.

William Greene was made a freeman, 1718, and was deputy, 1727, 32, 36, 38 and 40.

In 1728 William Greene and John Mumford were appointed surveyors of the line between Connecticut and Rhode Island. In October 1736, Daniel Abbott, John Jenkins and William Greene were appointed a committee on the line with Connecticut, and reported Nov. 20, 1739. [R. I. Col. Rec., vol. 4, p. 563-4.]

He was Deputy Governor in 1740, 42 and 43, and Governor in 1743, 44, 46, 48 to 55 and 57, eleven years.

The fact that a resident of Warwick was made Governor at all, in those days of the undisputed preponderance of Newport, proves, in itself, the importance of William Greene in the councils of the colony. Newport is frequently referred to in the records as our Metropolis; all the commerce was at Newport and all the public offices, and whether in peace or war, the bulk of colonial business, at that time, had reference to maritime affairs. From Sept. 1654 to May 1657, Roger Williams was President of the colony. From that time to 1743 (86 years) no Governor, not a resident of Newport, had been elected, except Joseph Jenckes, and he was required to move to Newport and the Assembly voted £100 for the expense of his removal. He served five years, from 1727 to 1732. There is no indication that the same thing was required of William Greene, though it is well known that John Greene had declined the honor with the condition.

Governor Greene's service was not continuous but with frequent intervals ; he died in the office at a not very advanced age. His intermittent occupation of it, over a space of fifteen years, is sufficient evidence that he showed himself worthy the confidence that first led to his selection. I presume he was selected because politics had not then become such an exact science as now, when candidates have to be suppressed instead of being sought out, and fitness is the last qualification required.

During the service of Governor Greene, the long contest, or series of contests, between the English and French, for the supremacy on this continent, which concluded by the conquest by the former of the French Provinces, was carried on with great vigor. A large amount of correspondence, between him and various royal officers, may be seen in the Colonial Records; they are not of a controversial character. On his part they are indicative of sterling sense and business-like talents.

During this time the long controversy between Rhode Island on the one part, and Plymouth and Massachusetts on the other part (Plymouth being now merged in Massachusetts), was concluded in 1747, by the annexation of five towns to Rhode Island, viz. : Cumberland, Warren, Bristol, Little Compton and Tiverton. Undoubtedly Governor Greene had been active and earnest in the matter, as would be, naturally, a grandson of John Greene, 2d, but his name was not conspicuous in it. It was a marvellous result, considering the character of our claim, and the magnitude of the obstacles to be overcome.

In 1745 Louisbourg and Cape Breton were taken by the English, the colonies aiding largely, and Rhode Island in full proportion, with ships and men. The invasion of England, by Charles Edward, occurred.

In 1746, Battle of Culloden and defeat of Pretender.

In 1747, French defeated at Belle-isle and Cape Finisterre.

In 1748, Peace of Aix la Chapelle.

In 1749, English settle Nova Scotia.

In 1752, New style introduced, and hostilities between English and French, on the boundaries of Nova Scotia.

In 1754, Washington's mission to the French.

In 1755, Braddock's defeat.

In 1758, Abercrombie's defeat at Ticonderoga.

In this contest the colonies gave all the aid in their power; and Governor Greene's letters show that every nerve was on extreme tension in Rhode Island, and every heart earnest for success. The colony became largely indebted for supplies, &c., furnished the government, all of which was expected to be reimbursed, and for which expenditures, large amounts of paper money were issued by the colony. Small part of this claim on the British government was ever realized. On the plea of the damage done Dr. Moffat and others, in the stamp act riots, in 1765, in Newport, and the destruction of the Gaspee and the failure of the colony to give satisfaction for them, no payments were thereafter made to the colony; and this burden was added to the heavy load which the Revolution occasioned, and was very prejudicial to the credit of the state, for a long period after its close. In fact, we may acknowledge, with some degree of shame, that our state treated some of its Revolutionary obligations in a manner not deserving a much milder term than repudiation.

The principal subject of interest during Governor Greene's administration, aside from the prosecution of the war, was the issue of bills of credit by the colony, which, under a delusion not yet quite without votaries, had induced the colony, as well as other colonies, to pledge their credit to a very large amount, so that it had become burdensome and alarming; under the idea that such issues, to any amount, loaned on real estate securities, would be safe and wholesome; experience proved it far otherwise. But questions of this sort are daily discussed by infinitely abler pens, and I forbear to discuss this subject further.

Governor Greene lies buried on the homestead which he inherited and which was originally set off to Samuel Gorton in the

Coheset division of lands in Warwick, near the East Greenwich line, now occupied by his great grandson, Hon. William Greene, late Lieutenant Governor of the state. The homestead has, therefore, never been alienated from the blood of Gorton.

SECOND GOVERNOR WILLIAM GREENE.

FIFTH GENERATION.

The second Governor William Greene was son of the first Governor William and his wife Catherine, daughter of Benjamin and Susanna (Holden) Greene, his grandmother being a daughter of Randall Holden.

He was born August 16, 1731, and died November 29, 1809. His wife was Catharine Ray, daughter of Simon and Deborah (Greene) Ray of Block Island, and granddaughter of Job Greene, son of John 2d by whose wife Phebe, daughter of John and Mary (Williams) Sayles, his descendants derive a strain from the blood of Roger Williams.

He was admitted free, May 1753.

In October 1771 he was on a committee with Thomas Aldrich to finish the Court House in East Greenwich.

In August 1772 he was appointed by the Assembly as a director of a lottery for the benefit of John Greene & Co., Griffin Greene and Nathaniel Greene & Co., ironworks, whose buildings had been burned.

He was Deputy from Warwick, 1773, 74, 76 and 77.

In February 1776 he was, with many others, on a committee to procure gold and silver coin for the expedition into Canada.

17

July 18, 1776. The Assembly, after accepting the Declaration of Independence, and ordering it proclaimed with suitable demonstrations and voting, " That the style and title of this government shall be, The State of Rhode Island and Providence Plantations." Voted " That the sheriff of the county of Newport, be ordered to take into his custody Edward Thurston of Newport, and that Messrs. George Sears, Jonathan Arnold, Jonathan Hassard, William Greene and Cromwell Child, be a committee to proceed, with the said sheriff, to the dwelling house of the said Edward Thurston, and there to demand of him that he open to their view all the desks or other suspected places under lock or otherwise, and if he shall refuse to show and unlock the same that the said committee be, and hereby is, directed to break open the same, and carefully to inspect and make search for any and all letters of correspondence upon the disputes between the independent states of America and Great Britain, or of a political nature, and such letters and papers as they shall think proper to bring with them for the inspection of this General Assembly."

A like vote was passed in relation to the papers of Daniel Coggeshall with same committee.

In August 1776 William Greene was elected 1st Associate Justice of the superior court, Metcalf Bowler being Chief Justice ; the others were Shearjashub Bourne, Jabez Bowen and Thomas Wells, Esquires.

December 10, 1776, he was chosen one of the council of war, the enemy having taken possession of Rhode Island.

In May 1777 he was elected speaker of the House of Representatives.

In October 1777 he was again appointed of the council of war.

In February 1778 he was made Chief Justice superior court.

In May 1778 he was installed Governor, being the second Governor of the state, and succeeding Governor Nicholas Cooke, who was the incumbent at the declaration of independence. This office he filled until May 1786, eight years.

In October 1792 he was an elector of President and Vice President of the United States and was, therefore, a member of the first electoral college in which Rhode Island participated.

A mass of correspondence between Governor Greene and the delegates in Congress and other parties may be found in the Colonial Records and in Mr. Staples' book, entitled Rhode Island in the Continental Congress, edited by Reuben Guild, Esq. All this is characterized by unwavering patriotism and by eminent ability. The bow, constantly strung during that trying period, never relaxed; how trying we can hardly now conceive.

We must imagine a population of less than 50,000, one-third of them, for several years, driven from their homes and thrown upon the other party for shelter and support; one quarter, and that the best, of the cultivable land in possession of the enemy; by sea, cut off from supplies by the cruisers of the foe, and on land, by embargoes on the part of the neighboring states; with a currency so depreciated as at one time to require $100 to be equivalent to two and a half dollars in money or any valuable commodity; in addition to these things a large part of the male population, engaged in the army or in armed vessels, and the remainder, constantly on the watch for incursions from an enemy, vastly superior, lying within sight of them and provided with all the appliances that the most formidable nation on earth could afford.

The most vivid imagination, with all these realities before it, can hardly form any adequate picture of the distresses of the people, all of which must of necessity have constantly wrung the heart of him to whom, as head of the government, all looked for succor. Calm, strong, immovable, he passed through that cruel ordeal with a reputation for wisdom and integrity accorded to but few men, even in that period of exceptional superiority.

Want of space precludes any thorough analysis of Governor Greene's career, which could only be worthily treated in an extensive publication.

Governor Greene's children were

Ray, married Mary M. Flagg, of George, Esq., of Charleston, South Carolina.

Samuel, married Mary Nightingale, of Colonel Joseph, of Providence, R. I.

Phebe, married Colonel Samuel Ward, of Governor Samuel, her cousin.

Celia, married Colonel William Greene, of Benjamin of Warwick Neck, her cousin.

HONORABLE RAY GREENE.

SIXTH GENERATION.

———

The eldest son of Governor Greene was the Hon. Ray Greene, who graduated at Yale college, and studied law in the office of General ·James M. Varnum in East Greenwich. He succeeded William Channing, Esq., as Attorney General of Rhode Island in 1794, which position he retained until October 1797, when he was elected to succeed Hon. William Bradford in the Senate of the United States. This place he resigned in May 1801, and his failure of health precluded his fulfilling any public duties thereafter.

HONORABLE WILLIAM GREENE.

—

His son, Hon. William Greene of Warwick, who now occupies the ancestral estate, graduated at Brown University, and having studied law at Litchfield, settled in Ohio about 1820, where most of his active life was passed. He returned to his early home in 1862, from which time he has been a resident of Rhode Island. In 1871 and 72 he was elected Lieutenant Governor of the state. He is the last male descendant of the second Governor Greene.

During his residence of forty years in Cincinnati he was prominent in the social and business circles of that city, and contributed largely, by his earnestness and energy, to the establishment of their excellent public schools and of the sytem of roads which, before the era of railways, gave the original impetus to the remarkable growth of that beautiful city.

ERRATA.

20th page, 9th line—Insert, after "Government," "or to impartial arbitrators, and it is due to the" (line omitted).

43d page, 1st line—For "now popular" read "non popular".

52d page, 21st line—For "wrested" read "wrestled".

www.ingramcontent.com/pod-product-compliance
Lightning Source LLC
Chambersburg PA
CBHW021527270326
41930CB00008B/1131